MILLION DOLLAR MINDSET PRESENTS

HOW TO WRITE A SUCCESSFUL BUSINESS PLAN

by LINKED IN AND TOWN HALL ACHIEVER OF THE YEAR

EY NOMINEE ENTREPRENEUR OF THE YEAR

GRAND HOMAGE LYS DIVERSITY

Dr. BAK NGUYEN, DMD

& Guest Author

ROUBA SAKR, BANKER

TO ALL OF THOSE DREAMING OF BUILDING THEIR OWN BUSINESS, HERE IS HOW TO COMMUNICATE WITH YOUR BANKS AND INVESTORS. HAVE THE MEANS OF YOUR DREAMS, WRITING THE RIGHT WORDS AND CONVEYING THE RIGHT EMOTIONS.

by Dr. BAK NGUYEN

ISBN: 978-1-989536-21-6

MILLION DOLLAR MINDSET PRESENTS

HOW TO WRITE A SUCCESSFUL BUSINESS PLAN

by Dr. BAK NGUYEN & guest author ROUBA SAKR

INTRODUCTION
BY Dr. BAK NGUYEN

PART I:
THE ENTREPRENEURIAL SPIRIT

FINDING YOUR ANGLE
CHAPTER 1- Dr. BAK NGUYEN
THE 7 RULES OF BUSINESS

THE FIRST STONE
CHAPTER 2- Dr. BAK NGUYEN
A WEBSITE IS YOUR FIRST MOVE

THE NUMBERS
CHAPTER 3 - Dr. BAK NGUYEN
FEELINGS CAN BE TRANSPOSED IN NUMBERS

THE STRUCTURE
CHAPTER 4 - Dr. BAK NGUYEN
SHORT' CONCISE, STRAIGHT TO THE POINT

THE EXPERTS
CHAPTER 5 - Dr. BAK NGUYEN
DON'T BE CHEAP, PUT ALL THE ODDS IN YOUR FAVOR

PART II:
THE BANKER'S MINDSET

INTRODUCTION
"BUILDING A DREAM"
by Dr. BAK NGUYEN

I am celebrating 2 years writing in 7 days, 7 days before the end of August. 24 months ago, I started my journey as a writer because I needed to prepare to speak on stage. Writing a chapter at the time, a book after the next, I found myself, my voice and much confidence.

I also introduced the art to my child of 8 a few months ago. Now at 9, he has co-signed 20 books with me, children's books. So am I proud? I will say more surprised than proud. Am I relentless? I will say that I am growing tired... but I can't stop!

At least not now that every newly written book is a new world record! About that, the world record, I haven't been recognized as such yet, I haven't even submitted, too busy writing and pushing the publishing.

So here are the results after 23 months and 3 weeks: 47 titles written (listed at the end of this book), 22 titles available for download on Apple Books and 8 available for print-on-demand from Amazon.

The same 8 are available on Kindle for download, and soon to be lived, one **EAX (Enhanced Audio Experience)**, an audiobook blockbuster, making reading cool again!

You might say that this is quite impressive. What impressed you, intimidate me. If I knew what I was in for, I would probably never had done it. This has been a discovery to you and me, almost simultaneously, me writing, you reading.

I will continue to write for as long as the words are still coming to me. That, I promise. I will keep publishing and empower other authors to write for as long as I still have a book to publish and an author to inspire. But mainly, I have been able to do as much because I have a structure.

A structure to write, one to edit, another to publish. Now it is the time for the sale team to kick in. All different exercise and skillset. Distribution and sale are not the same as production.

Once again, I started this journey for the fun of it, not to get tangled in the process and to learn new protocols. But to last, I follow my own templates, and once I got the right tuning, I kept repeating the template again and again. That's for the shape, the content is a whole other story.

I know about my template and process writing books, I wrote **HOW TO WRITE A BOOK IN 30 DAYS** a few months back, giving you the exact step I follow writing and keep writing. That was number 40 and the first title in the **MILLION DOLLAR**

MINDSET series, names after my Podcast. The series is mainly a series of **HOW TO** book.

My 46th book was pushed by my marketing team, **HOW TO NOT FAIL AS A DENTIST**, delivering my understanding and knowledge from 20 years+ in the field, serving on the frontline. A **HOW-TO** book dedicated to dentists, especially the newly graduate.

In a word, I gave in a book what I am telling my dentists on the floor, and in 20 years, I have mentored more than one dentist. The book is only the first step.

They made me promise to commit to the recording a seminars series covering the subject in depth. Within the next months, all my colleagues' dentists will have access to my secrets and template for the profession.

Then, I went on vacation in California, reconnecting with myself of 18 years ago, hesitating between **Hollywood** and **Dentistry**. This time, I got more answers than questions. It also gave life to **HORIZON Volume 2, On the footsteps of Titans**.

The **Horizon series** was my response to all those requests to have an insight into my lifestyle and of how I forged my mindset. I have to tell you that I was skeptic at first and a little resistant to the idea of sharing my lifestyle, not because of secrecy, but because I couldn't see the interest in doing so.

The fans and the marketing experts were pushing for story and pictures to post on Instagram. That something else that I do not fully understand, Instagram. But why argue when I do not understand. I took the demands and rendered what I could: through a book, then, two.

Today the **Horizon series** is one of my favourites to write. Oh, and I almost forgot, I got 8 books published on Amazon (available in the paperback version) and have managed to gain the credibility with both Amazon and Apple to have my book approved within days. At Apple, it is now a matter of hours.

Exhaustive, won't you agree? Yesterday, I had a few corporate meeting, and I also understood the need to have a second Dr. Bak's event, maybe under the umbrella of **Mdex** as a Mdex's Keynote to address the world and our partners about the progression of the company.

I have large shoulders and can swallow much and quickly. I will be up to the task. This will have to take place within the next month, month and a half at most, on top of my existing project. So once again, how do I manage?

Them, I realize that I only have a little more than a week before the celebration of 2 years of writing. In other words, if I want to have my **48 books / 24 months**, I will have to start and finish yet another book within a week or so.

The last time that I face that kind of deadline was we I reached **15 books / 15 months**, last by November 2018. I remembered how hard it was and how tired and clueless I was. But I did it! Record or not, no one can take that away from my ledger!

Then, I started writing with my son William. By the beginning of March, it wasn't planned, but he helped me to show **36 books / 18 months + 1 week**. That was simply amazing and surprising. I hated the **+1 week**, but it is what it is.

This cornerstone of 24 months is my chance to set a new world record, 48 books / 24 months, a marathon of sprints considering that each book took 2-3 weeks in average, that's the sprint. To do it again and again over the last 24 months is the marathon.

I am a sprinter, **Momentum** is my power, never would I know that I could be a marathoner. I am very aware of the level of concentration and discipline that my condition now requires. It is no hobby anymore!

False, I am simply doing it for the fun of it, and I may add, I love the vibe of impressing, not only the people, but myself.

So I went online and asked my fan base what they would like to read next from me. Building a business and **HOW TO**… were high on the priority demands.

So this is it. I bring to you **HOW TO WRITE A SUCCESSFUL BUSINESS PLAN** my 48th book. In the fashion of the **MILLION DOLLAR MINDSET series**, I will deliver to you my template and mindset building a business.

I will cover both the launch of a small enterprise as I did so many times within 20 years of entrepreneurship but also include part of what I am experiencing right now and I am launching a bluechip company, asking for millions of dollars in loans and investments.

Even I mentioned **HOW TO WRITE A SUCCESSFUL BUSINESS PLAN**, this book will be mostly about how to launch an enterprise. The business plan part was to make sure that you will have something tangible by the end of this reading.

Also, I will invite a good friend of mine to join this book, banker Rouba Sakr. To every story, this is two sides, Rouba will be sharing with you the banker's side of the finance. And wait for it, are you ready? I am waved her non-disclosure on the matter of the business plan of **Mdex & Co**.

For the first time, you will have within the same book, both the version of the entrepreneur and the banker to complete the story and have a clear vision of what is it to be in business and to ask for money.

"You know that you've reached Momentum
the day it is easier to continue than to stop."
Dr. Bak Nguyen

This is where I am: in the **EYE** of my **Momentum**, inspired and tired all at once. I am as tired as I am excited to be sharing, once again with you.

With the experience and the knowledge within this book, all of you will have the means to put on paper your vision and to have a chance to partner up with the financial institution in order to leverage words into reality.

"To leverage your words into reality,
it is sharing, not selling."
Dr. Bak Nguyen

This is the **MILLION DOLLAR MINDSET.**

Dr. BAK NGUYEN

PART I
THE ENTREPRENEURIAL SPIRIT
by Dr. BAK NGUYEN

CHAPTER 1
"FINDING YOUR ANGLE"
by Dr. BAK NGUYEN

The first thing when it comes to business is to have an idea. Obvious? Not really. If you think that by having an idea, even a great one, is enough to open a business, be prepared to be heavily tested and challenged.

The first thing in business is to respond to a need. In other words, you need to identify your market, your customers.

After 20 years in entrepreneurship, I will tell you that to identify your market and the need you are fulfilling is the single most crucial aspect of your business plan.

Even if you have created a marvel of technology that people have no use for or do not understand, you might hold on to that invention for a long, long time.

> "To serve a solution,
> that's the core of a business."
> **Dr. Bak Nguyen**

A solution, in other words, you need to identify the problem, to you and your audience clearly. Then, by targeting that specific problem, you can then propose a new solution (your business proposal) to fix the situation or to improve on an inefficient solution. This is identifying your need.

We might all think that to create a new need and to create a new market is the sexiest thing to do. True, for the narrative and the glory... if you are ready to spend millions on marketing and public relation.

Everyone likes to hear about a new revolutionary gadget. Will they buy it? Most people won't until their peers all have adapted to it.

So to create a brand new market is much more complicated than one might think.

"Forget the sexiness,
embrace the efficacy instead."
Dr. Bak Nguyen

This is why everyone has a chance in business. You do not need to be a genius to be successful, to follow some basic ground rules:

- identify a specific need
- identify your market

- present your solution and its edge (quality, price, availability…)
- deliver what you promise
- make sure of a distribution system
- have a good management
- control your cost (profitability)

Those **seven rules** are some of the most important ground rules to start in business. We covered the first one already. Now, about the second one, identifying your market.

What is the difference between identifying a need and identifying a market? A need is what it is, a void in the market to respond adequately to a task. A market is the people aware and ready to pay to obtain such a solution. Trust a need is not a market, but not at all.

"Never confuse a need for a market."
Dr. Bak Nguyen

Even if people need something, if they do not know how to apply the solution that you are proposing, your business is doomed to fail, unless you spend millions to convince and educate them.

If people do not care about their need, your business will fail, unless you spend millions to educated them. If people do not have the money to buy such a solution, you can spend the millions in marketing, and you will still go bankrupt.

Of course, you will need to spend on marketing, to announce to the world the is a new and better solution available to them, but then, if you have identified your market successfully, they might buy right away. You were merely there to show them where to buy, not to convince them.

I just summarized to you modern marketing. Nowadays, with the social media and the paid AdWords, you have the means to target the specific segment of the population would act on such proposal. The more accurate your targeting, the cheaper your marketing cost.

This confirmed **rule #2**, to identify your market, even before you have found a unique business proposal to sell to them.

"More important than to know what you are selling is to know who you are talking to."
Dr. Bak Nguyen

Rule #3, the solution. This is where most entrepreneurs will start from, to invent something new. I must clarify, you do not need to create anything to be in business, although some of the most successful business people have developed something unique.

That's what you heard in the narrative and the documentary because this is where a story is gaining in weight and appeal.

Look at the business scene, some of the wealthiest and most successful business people haven't invented anything new, they have mastered a system: the distribution system.

In other words, you may have invented a great tool. It is now on you to convince the world of its usefulness and believe me; people do not like to change the habits, especially the bad ones.

On that, you can trust me; I am a doctor in dental medicine, I do not sell, I treat. I have the authority to prescribe treatments, surgery, and drugs.

And even when people are in pain, they are looking for a quick fix, not a reorganization of their lifestyle. This is where most inventors miss the track completely.

On the other hand, if you have found a way to improve upon an existing product, the game may sound more complicated since you have a competitor.

Once again, trust me, you have a better opportunity since the market has already been identified and formed for you. All you need to do now is to target that same demography and to tell them how your solution is a better one.

It can be more efficient, last longer, more environment-friendly, more affordable, more available. Whatever weakness the leader of the market has, you can now exploit as a selling point. It might even sound as if you are cheating…

The cheat was that you did not have to create the market nor to educate them. You are getting in the game at a different stage, one where people are already buying. The only question is from who they will be buying.

To ensure a favorable answer to the last question, make sure to check as many advantages as possible (price, quality, efficiency, availability…)

Now **rule #4**, this is the most obvious of them all, but too often it is the main flaw of most entrepreneur's proposal. Deliver what you have promised!

This rule has two component, to deliver and to promise. If you miss one of the two ingredients, you have lost your target and your sales' numbers. Let me explain.

Of course, your product has to be as expected and even better. It has to do the work, and help people to improve on their lives not create more hassles to untangled.

Unfortunately, we can all tell a story where what we bought caused us more despairs and time that what it was meant to solve as a solution. That's the delivering part.

But what to expect and what was the promise to beginning with? This is where branding and marketing will prove to be critical ingredients in the success of a product.

You need to get a clear message out to your customers, so they know that you exist and they know what to expect.

Only then, if they buy, they can testify to the validity of your solution. You have spoons at home. You are using them every day. If the brake or, the possibility will be more than you have lost them, you will buy some to replace those broken or lost spoons.

Depending on the budget that you had in mind, the quality of the material, the refinement and the price will dictate your choice. What was the brand that you bought? Often, you do not know, do not remember or don't even care.

On the same principles, so is the buying of a new TV screen. But why is it that you know what is the "name" of your TV? I have a SAMSUNG 65 inch or a new Sony 70 inch?

What was the difference between the TV and the spoon? Price, of course, but trust me, I have seen spoons more expensive than TVs.

The difference is that the brand of a TV will procure you a sense of belonging; this is the top quality or of the latest technology available.

The spoons, they were a commodity. And think of it for a moment, we have more useful use of the spoons daily than of the TVs.

That's the promise.

"Make a bold promise and keep it.
That's the key to any relationship,
especially in business."

Dr. Bak Nguyen

Now **rule #5**, make sure of your distribution process. This rule is not as simple as it might sound. If you have successfully implement your marketing and production in place, people with still need to know where to buy it.

Nowadays, online e-commerce is your best bet, since people can take immediate action between their emotion that they want what you have to offer and the ordering. Make sure that the process is as smooth and friendly as possible.

You can also have them available in stores. Once again, it's a duo, to have the marketing and the distribution dancing in harmony one with the other.

Spend too much on marketing without distribution, you have created a wasted opportunity and maybe even worse, frustration from your clients.

Spend too much time on the distribution process without proper marketing coverage and your products will be sleeping on the shelves, testing your resolves, your patience, and the depth of your pocket.

It is a well balanced and well-thought decision-making process that will ensure your success. This is more than distribution; it is management.

Management is such a big word, one in which we throw in all the business tasks that do not have a specific label. I will recognize it; management has a branding problem. But besides that, management is a crucial factor in any business.

We talked about mastering a system, well that's the role of management. Management is not only the mastering of one system but the mastering and dancing of the many different methods that will keep a business relevant for the years to come. Management that was **rule #6**.

Now **rule #7**, control your cost. Profit is what left from the sales' numbers after all the expenses. There is no point doing business when you spend more to get your products out than what you bring in.

Obvious no? Not so much.

As a business, you will always be spending first and more than what you will bring in. Eventually, you will have to refine your equations to balance it out and to make up also for the initial lost you have encountered.

The equation goes like this: the more you spend smartly, the more people will know about it, the more units you will sell.

That is only if you have spent enough to produce them at the beginning. So you spent a lot of money before selling your first unit.

Let's say that you have miscalculated a step and you are short of liquidity. What do you cut, the production (that took much time to assemble and to train... again money, money, money?) or the marketing that cost much, but is directly related with your sales' numbers?

You see the delicate balance, always walking on the edge? This is the world of a business owner and the decision-makers in a corporation.

It is never noticeable and never do we have all of the answers; the only thing we can be is to be prepared.

"To be prepared,
this is the essence of a business plan."
Dr. Bak Nguyen

Any veteran business person will know that whatever is written in your business plan is not set in stone, but at least, you have given it a thought and know at least, that part of the journey.

Whatever may happen, you have the experience of going through a scenario once, and if you have act soon enough, may have the chance to readjust and to course-correct your actions and business decisions.

"Business is not about being right,
but much more about being tuned."
Dr. Bak Nguyen

This will require much attention and flexibility from the decisions makers. To be tuned with your market is the only way for a business to last and to flourish.

To be tuned and to be prepared, the first step is to have a business plan, one that you have to spend time and effort polishing and understanding. Not one that you have paid a firm for.

Wealth and success are about mindset. So many times, you wondered how to build a successful mindset. This is step one, spend time to prepare, and to develop your business plan. Doing so, you are also making your business case.

To succeed, one needs more than
a genius idea; one needs a plan. "
Dr. Bak Nguyen

This is the **MILLION DOLLAR MINDSET.**

GIVE YOURSELF THE MEANS OF YOUR VISION,
THIS TIME, STAY IN THE BOX, MASTER THE TABLE.

Dr. BAK NGUYEN

CHAPTER 2
"THE FIRST STONE"
by Dr. BAK NGUYEN

Ready to start? I can share your excitement. So do it, right away, today! Yup, you heard me right, do something today, as we speak.

Business is a matter of preparation and planning, but that does not mean that one can be spontaneous and have fun, in real-time. You can start writing your business plan. Nowadays, I think that there are better ways to starts. Here's mine:

I start by doing my website. To secure a name.com will be an adventure on its own since most dot com have been taken already. That will force your mind to start flexing.

Remember, the only reality in business is that things are always changing and no matter your plans, you will have to adapt. Start to integrate that in your DNA, from the start.

Secure a cool .com and go on, build your website. Just like the business plan, a website can be a technical challenge for many. I started when one had to code to build a website.

Nowadays, a website can be built in a matter of hours and without any coding.

Web platforms like **SQUARESPACE** and **WIX** will allow anyone; I mean anyone to build a beautiful website from their templates within the day. I'd start with that if I were you. I fact, I envy you since it is so much easier today to start a business.

Once again, you heard right, a website is the beginning of your journey, building your business. Remember **Rule #1** and **Rule #2**, to identify a **need** and a **market**? Well, the easiest thing to test those is with a website.

You can write the best business plan ever; only a few will look at it, even if they are the famous people making the decisions, you still need to fly on your own.

In other words, by testing your idea out there, in the wild of the web, you are proving your concept and building credibility.

"In business, the single most important person is the customer."

Dr. Bak Nguyen

And the beauty of it, there are billions of customers out there. Reach out for them. In that sense, your website is your anchor, a place where you can clearly explain what you are offering and to whom.

Marketing people will say that we are doing things in reverse. They might be right, but they also have a process called market reach and focus group on testing an idea. Usually, those are also conducted at the first steps of the launch of any new product.

You might not have the millions supporting them, but you can beat your timeline by combining business plan, market reach, and PR campaign.

"A website is the best first move an entrepreneur can take."

Dr. Bak Nguyen

Cost-wise, don't be too cheap, go for those $20 to $40 a month subscription plan, since it will allow you the access to the real tools and power of a website: data gathering, premium design, and social media sharing tools.

It used to cost tens of thousands of dollar and months to build a website, put things in perspective, and forget that free trial mentality.

"Forget the free meal. There is no such thing in business unless you are eating a bait."
Dr. Bak Nguyen

As I told you many times over by now, time is the essence and the most valuable resource you have at your disposal. But standing far from all those free trials, you are merely saving yourself much precious time trying this and this. Choose one that fits your needs and invest in it.

Once again, I will strongly recommend you to build your website. Not for the sake of saving, but for the purpose of practicing your speech and refining your ideas.

You know that you will have to adapt your concept and to react to the public and their comments.

"Flexibility does not mean to be spineless.
It means to be confident enough
to listen and to please."
Dr. Bak Nguyen

Yes, to please. So from the name of the website, you now will have to choose a theme and colors.

Even if you will later have experts to redesign the whole thing, do the first step yourself and start that romance with your creation. If you feel any emotion coming out of the process, your visitors may pick up on the vibes too.

To gain your first customer will always be the hardest of tasks. The only way I know how to appeal to a customer is from the heart.

So yes, you will need a beautiful design and a color theme that matches your brand. You are designing your **brand** at this stage.

What is your **promise** to the public? What is the **feel** of your company? Who are you? Why should they **trust** you? Those are all fundamental questions that you will have to answer writing a business plan.

In a website, they are the forefront of your site, at least until you have many lines of product to present.

A website is composed of 3 mains ingredients:

- a structure (template bought from the platform)
- images (which you can either purchase or use your own)
- texts (your ideas)

If you have followed the steps, the first two components could be obtained within a few clicks and with a budget in the hundreds of dollar... which is the best deal available if you are considering seriously to go in business.

A meeting with the right marketing agency will have cost you as much!

Eventually, you might add a fourth ingredient to the mix, **videos**. Those you will have to shoot yourself or have a professional team to do it.

But for now, forget the videos, start with getting your website online with a .com and the first page: to whom, why, and what are you selling. Then, you may add: **who you are and why you are well suited to help them**.

Do that in that **specific order**, just not to get lost in the details. Who you are is the least of their concerns (even if it is essential for the closing of the sale).

"You are just in the preludes of your relationship with your customers, it is about them, all about them."

Dr. Bak Nguyen

I will advise you to use fewer words as possible to describe to **WHOM** and **WHY**. Then, you arrived at **WHAT YOU ARE SELLING**; you can give more details.

The logic is simple. Nowadays, people have a short attention span; we are taking off minutes, even seconds. You want to be bold, precise and straight to the point.

"Logic will take many words to explain, go for the emotions instead."

Dr. Bak Nguyen

This is how the imagery of the website will help you to appeal to emotions and reduce the number of words before you connect with a person.

HEY, YOU is not the right choice of words, but the intention is exactly what you want to convey. ARE YOU TIRED OF… is the best opening line to hook with your public.

Know who you are talking to, your target audience. Have that target audience in the image, one reflecting the emotion who wish to appeal to.

For example, **MOMS ARE YOU TIRED OF KIDS BEING CLUED TO THEIR TABLETS?** - with the picture of a MOM reading peacefully to her daughter - this will be a great opening line to sell a new book.

Then, have it followed by **IT IS TIME FOR YOU TO RETAKE CONTROL AND TO HAVE SOME QUALITY TIME WITH YOUR KIDS**. This will be your promise and the refinement of your audience.

Two phrases and two images. The second one could be one where the mom and the kids are laughing together, maybe hugging with a sunset background.

The emotions are there, the promise well felt, and now, it is for you to deliver! Two images, 28 words within two phrases. Total attention span: 15 seconds, 20 at most.

Those two can be separate images or combined into a small video montage of 20 seconds. Even those free applications from your smartphone will put those together.

Platforms like **SQUARESPACE** and **WIX** (and no, I am not sponsored by any of them) will help you through the messaging by replacing the imagery in their template with your message. The structure and the logic are pretty similar from one platform to the next.

If you want my opinion, I prefer to work with **SQUARESPACE** for their design and ease of use. I also like their logic, which is similar to the mind of an artist and less of an engineer.

If you should have a comparison is like **Apple's** mentality where it is about what you can do with a powerful tool, not about how it works.

Of course, there will be a learning curve, but from everything that I have experienced until now, the workflow of **SQUARESPACE** is the most intuitive, their designs are stunning, and the technology and the tools of SEO, social integration and DATA gathering are powerful, they often exceed my expectations.

But no matter the opinion, it all boils down to the ease of use, can you build a website with the hour and have fun doing so? We each have our personality and preference.

Once again, I will tell you how much I envy you since, in my days, I had an engineering team to do the same work... and without social media integration, SEO was the only game in town.

Even the SEO (search engine optimization) rules kept changing.

"Forget perfection; just have a draft done online as quickly as possible.
Then react and refine."
Dr. Bak Nguyen

Don't be surprised that you might revisit and redesign your website more than once. This is part of the process, and it is way cheaper both in money and time to work on a website than to change your business plan.

So after the two primary images and their promise, your third page will be the presentation of your solution: **WHAT ARE YOU**

SELLING? I am sure that this is the natural part for you.

If you have followed the steps and the chronological of this process, you will notice that writing your description; you have started to adapt your words according to the first two primary images, their emotions, and their promises.

That is precisely the purpose of the exercise. You can take the time to summarize and explain the pros of your product, now that you have your targeted audience's attention.

Have you noticed that your company name, logo, and history are not even relevant yet? Those might be of prime importance to you, but not as much to your public. Try always to see things from their perspective.

After you have presented your product, here comes the call to action, **BUY NOW!** This is where your company name and logo will have to convey a sense of security, of trustworthiness.

Add to it a landline and our physical address, and you are all set. Even if you have set up a production line nor any distribution yet, you can always receive an email telling you of a pre-order and to start building your mailing and ordering list.

If you must, you can also use platforms like **Kickstarter.com** or **Indigogo.com** that will allow you to have people pre-ordering and pre-paying for your product.

But you will still need a website first to establish your credibility. Those are crowdfunding websites and have grown very much in popularity, especially for tech startups.

About the imagery, most websites building platform will propose free images. If you must, you can buy royalty-free photos (purchase images for a commercial purpose) at sites like **Shutterstock.com** and **adobe stock photos** for premium pictures. There are also free public domain images you can find at **Pixabay.com** and **Pexels.com**.

Everything is within a few clicks, and you'll be surprised by what you can do within an hour. The words are yours, the coding, the structure, and the images can be easily found.

Are you still here or have you gone to build your website? Building a website is so easy nowadays that there is simply no valid excuse not to use the opportunity to test and to refine your ideas and business proposal.

In short, a website might and jump-started you and propel you into the business world even before you got your corporation recorded yet. It can be as fast.

"Think as you do, listen, and adapt.
This is the speed of today's business."
Dr. Bak Nguyen

With a website live, a mailing list growing daily, you have the experience to start writing your business plan. The significant part is that the introduction of your business plan will be copy-paste from the text on your website.

Only this time, your target audience has changed; you are now looking to convince a banker and potential investor, not a client anymore.

Identify their needs and our audience and adapt. It is mainly the same process you've been through with the website; you only have to adjust the wording and the numbers.

About the numbers, before, you might pull numbers from the sky. This time, you can look at your first experience and build from those number.

For example, you spent $100 in marketing for one week and got five pre-ordered sales and 15 emails. Simple math will be to invest 10K and have 500 pre-ordered deals and 1.5K emails.

It is not as accurate, and the accounting team will be more sophisticated, but they will have a figure to base their projection on.

You are many steps closer to building your business, merely after two chapters of **HOW TO WRITE A SUCCESSFUL BUSINESS PLAN**. Do you want to keep going?

This is the **MILLION DOLLAR MINDSET.**

GIVE YOURSELF THE MEANS OF YOUR VISION.
THIS TIME, STAY IN THE BOX, MASTER THE BOX.

Dr. BAK NGUYEN

CHAPTER 3

"THE NUMBERS"

by Dr. BAK NGUYEN

What were you hoping for? You are in business, and it always comes down to your numbers! For those of you who had some experience, you already know, numbers are not absolute!

Just like words can be used to tell a story, the numbers are used in the same way. In other words, you can make numbers tell the story that you want.

They are neither the truth nor the absolute. Numbers are, in business, a point of reference, one that you will be **accountable** for, but nothing more than a point of reference.

That is mainly why most visionary will tell you to think big and to go beyond your scope. You will have to pave the way to the sky anyway and doing so, will have to reinvent yourself and your tools more than once, so aim for something worth both your time and energy.

You can make a plan for one million, that is not harder than to make a plan for 10K. Actually, in my experience, it is harder to make a plan for 10K since the initial investment will be harder to justify and to recoup on such a small number.

In the scope of millions, sure you are taking more risks, but you will also have more room to maneuver and a buffer in the case that you are mistaken.

Anything of worth will take resources; if you are too scarce, you are heading for disaster.

"Don't be cheap nor chicken when it comes to defining your ambitions."
Dr. Bak Nguyen

My time and moral are the most valuable resources that I hold. I will be risking my reputation, spending my days and money on a project.

I do it because I see the vision. I do it because I believe in the project, I also do it because it is worth my time! So do not restrain yourself, see and far as your mind allows you. Then, reserved-engineer the path to the goal.

"Think big and deliver. That's my job."
Dr. Bak Nguyen

A great friend and mentor of mine, Dr. Jean De Serres wrote in a book co-signed with me that to have a 5 million dollar startup is a gamble. To have a 20 million dollar startup is a company.

And I have to add that the man is wise and much more conservative than I am when it is about taking the risk. Leave yourself room to breathe and to evolve.

So whatever dream you have, look beyond your horizon, look at the global market, and scale down from there. It is always easier to scale down than to scale up. Start with the **big picture**.

For example, you are looking to sell books. Do not merely multiply your prospect by a factor and build your business plan from there. That first test was simply a trial, one without depth, long term strategy, nor real budget.

Look at the number of books sold last year in the country. Narrow it down to the number of books in your category and then, run some comparison analysis (how much they spend on marketing, who are they targeting, how are they portraying the author…).

Based on those numbers, you can now elaborate on a feasible and realistic scenario of sale and expense. If the final numbers are too small for your ambitions, change your product, you won't be able to reinvent a market, at least not with credibility from the eyes of the financiers you are looking to convince.

Just like real-estate, financiers are used to comparing your ideas and enterprise with **comparables**.

The closest, the better. I told you from the start that you do not need to be a genius and to reinvent the wheel at every step to succeed in business. Just make sense, find logic and a market and stick to them, at least for the first few rounds.

"Stick with your logic and your market,
but listen to the market and adapt to their
demands if you want to last."
Dr. Bak Nguyen

So you know that you will have to deliver, that's your accountability, your credibility, and final destination. You also understand that sky is the limit... and maybe beyond, for as long as you have the shoulder to walk your talk.

Base your walk from the field and the size of the market you have targeted. Then, narrow down your objectives.

"It is easier to scale down than to scale up. While planning, leave room for the scaling down."

Dr. Bak Nguyen

The words might be the same or close enough, but only the numbers will differ depending on your ambitions and vision. The difference will be who will be surrounding you then.

"Make a stand and move forward from there, never looking back."

Dr. Bak Nguyen

What I meant by this is that now that you have clarified your number and the scope of your project, the reactions will start raining. Some of the experts will encourage you and tell you that you have a significant plan in hand.

Unfortunately, most of the expert surrounding you, your friends and family will all try to convince you to tune it down.

If your project were one of a kind, one that will change your life forever, all of those standing next to you wouldn't see it, since they are used to see you for who are were, not who you will grow into.

And then again, if your project does not have this kind of reactions, by experience, I might tell you to rethink your plans, since they might not be worth it. Anything of worth should change your situation, not just get you 10 or 20% ahead.

Is that greed? Absolutely not, this is vision. Reality is that you won't be ahead for a long time. For months and years, you might be way behind since you are investing everything that you have and are in your business.

"It is when you have invested everything
and that you have nothing that
the real growth kicks in."
Dr. Bak Nguyen

I am not saying that you should bet your house on the first move. I am merely saying that while you are drafting your plan, don't try to play it safe from the ambition standpoint. Leave yourself room to learn, to fail and to grow.

I don't think that any entrepreneur reaches their original goals by 100%. They might surpass them one day by an X factor, but always, to keep that hunger and determination to move forward, even when they are exhausted and wholly emptied, what they had in their heart was the rush to make up for their delays and setbacks.

"To the world, it might look like ambition;
to them, they were way behind, always.
This is the mindset of a champion
and an entrepreneur."
Dr. Bak Nguyen

What does that mean? It means that the numbers will change. No matter what you put down on paper, you will never be fully satisfied as an entrepreneur.

If you have exceeded your goal, you might celebrate for a day, but then, you might think that you were not ambitious enough.

"Smile and readjust. It's a new day;
it's a new game."
Dr. Bak Nguyen

Most of the time, you will fall behind your numbers. It is okay, for as long as you were still in the same scope. If you were talking about millions and are in the tens of thousand, that another story…

But if you had a good plan and have learned and adapted throughout your journey, you might not be as far behind.

Whatever is missing, add it to your next year target. You are putting more pressure on your system and yourself, that's how your numbers will scale up even when you were behind. That's how I operate to leverage from each of my failures.

Then, the new vibe is not even optimistic, and it is the frustration of the underdog lagging and coming back with all he got because it is the only way to come, with all that you have, even when you FINDING by failure.

You read often, and I am sure that success is a lousy teacher. In the case that you are successful, of course, the feeling is great, but how will you keep your focus and keep your troops committed? More than often, complacency will kick in and start eating up the joins of your team.

You may agree or disagree with me, but don't let pride blindside you while complacency kick in since it will be an illness worse than cancer to treat.

"To treat complacency often, amputation is the only remedy…"

Dr. Bak Nguyen

A most undesirable outcome! So trust me, leave yourself room to grow, make mistakes, and learn. Think big, write it down on paper and expand your mind until the numbers make sense.

If your counsels can't follow you, they can't assist you. Do not adapt yourself to them; find new counsel. When I said to adjust, adapt yourself to your market and customer, not to your aids. If they couldn't adapt to you, they have lost your business.

"Feelings can be transposed in words or numbers. Usually, the numbers will be of better uses."

Dr. Bak Nguyen

It happened more than once to me. I am a very loyal person, and it took me years and countless scar to understand that loyalty is to a cause, not a person. Be faithful to your mission and call, not to the people you meet on the way.

Be kind and generous to them. Be respectful and share the journey that your destinies and ambitions allow. But when it is time to depart, be courteous and wish them luck, you have too much to do ahead to look back, and so they are.

Do not have regrets, unless you know that you have done wrong, unnecessarily. If that's the case, repent, apologize and move forward. To make up for your mistake is not to stand behind, it is to speed up and to make up for the lost time and opportunity.

Following that same logic, most of the time, the person you have disappointed is no one but yourself. Make up for your mistake and compensate by growing, looking forward.

The title of this chapter was the **NUMBERS**. So to make sense of the feeling you are experimenting right now, put them down, not in words, but numbers. The bigger the numbers, the stronger the emotion.

Greed, fear, ambition, frustration, excitement, the words do not matter in here; only the numbers do. Then leverage on those feelings to react, to make sense of the numbers you put down on paper. Resist to the fact to erase and to write down a new number.

Until you have elaborate a plan to reach those initial numbers, do not be distracted by doubts, fears, or greed. I many if not most of my books; I am telling you to listen to yourself, well, this is listening to yourself. You heard, now act, do not second guess.

Be real, be honest, and let yourself go. The words may change; the numbers are your ladders in the mindset of an entrepreneur.
Write down. Yours.

This is the **MILLION DOLLAR MINDSET.**

GIVE YOURSELF THE MEANS OF YOUR VISION.
THIS TIME, STAY IN THE BOX, MASTER THE BOX.

Dr. BAK NGUYEN

CHAPTER 4
"THE STRUCTURE"
by Dr. BAK NGUYEN

Short, concise, and straight to the point. Can it be clearer? Know your audience! You are talking with business people, financier and investor, all people who understand the value of time.

They do not care much about the words. They care about the numbers, the ratio, and the presentation!

So now that you have the confidence of a test run from the building and launching of your **WEBSITE**, you know your message and promise to the public. You have your **PROMISE** and your **MARKET**.

You also figured out your ambitions and how your **PROMISE** will impact the world. Those are the basis of your **NUMBERS**. You know that your **NUMBERS** have to express and cause feelings. That's how you'll get an appealing and authentic **NARRATIVE**.

The story that your **NUMBERS** are telling is your **NARRATIVE**. And your **NARRATIVE** is the spine of your account and speech to the bankers and investors.

So to summarize, you have:

- **PROMISE (NEEDS & SOLUTION)**
- **MARKET (WHO will be buying)**
- **NUMBERS (the scale of your AMBITIONS and enterprise and numbers of the Global market.)**
- **NARRATIVE (the plan of how you will grow those NUMBERS)**

That will also be your structure writing a business plan. The first draft should be comprised within 4-8 pages. Then, just like your **WEBSITE**, you might add some extra useful information as:

- WHO is the team behind (and a short resumé)
- An analysis of the other players in the same market
- contact information

This wasn't the way that I wrote my business plan. But reading those business proposals from companies seeking investment, New York, Toronto, Montreal, they all have the same structure: 4-8 pages and seven mains sections:

- PROMISE (Words)
- MARKET (Graph)
- NUMBERS (Words)
- NARRATIVE (Graph)
- TEAM (Picture)
- CONTACT INFO

Often, in shorter versions, the **MARKET** also included the analysis and the competitors. The quicker, the better. This is why I gave you a code system to know what is the critical points of each section.

In the **PROMISE** section, use words to establish the needs you have identified and what you propose to solve it. You can reuse the exact strategy and wording that you used on your **WEBSITE**.

WHAT - TO WHOM

You might have 20 seconds again to appeal to the interest. Mainly, it is about the wording in here, short, concise, and straight to the point wording. That should be half of a page, to the most, your first page.

Then, the **MARKET**. Identify the market you are aiming for. Start with the Global size of the market and its potential. Then, quickly zoom in to your segment of the market and provide essential numbers.

HOW BIG - HOW MUCH

Business people love to be educated and to receive insight into the **MARKET**. By giving them ideas, you are talking their tongue; in other words, you are relating to them.

Be careful of the numbers that you are showing since they will challenge you on them. That's normal; it is how business people create connection and assert the quality of the people they meet.

You should have a pie illustrating the market and the different segment and a graph to show the potential of the global market.

Just like the imagery you used to convey emotions on your **WEBSITE**, the graph and pie in this section will ease and appeal to your audience (**FINANCIERS**) to feel home. It there is a feeling you want to convey out of this is **SECURITY** and familiarity.

If they trust you, they might read further.

"To have the interest of a FINANCIER, they must first trust you."
Dr. Bak Nguyen

That's what you are trying to establish by the second page of your business plan, **TRUST**. Use the **MARKET** to develop that trust and make sure that you have the explanation to justify the figures and numbers you are showing.

Then, we come to the critical part of the business plan, the **NUMBERS**, your numbers. In this section is where you announce the scope of your enterprise, the profit, and the growth potential.

Even if the section is named **NUMBERS**, except some prominent figures, it will mainly constitute of words. What should be bold and evident is the size and scope of your proposal. You may present some ratio too.

The **NUMBERS** section is a business card. Now that you have the interest of the **FINANCIERS**, they want to know who you are. Not in the usual sense of where you went to school and what you've achieved… not yet. They want to know if listening to you is worth their time.

WHO I AM - WHY WE SHOULD PARTNER UP

Your **NUMBERS** will be telling them if you are worth their time. Remember, a business plan is mainly the prelude for a conversation with the decision-makers.

Have it right, and you will have a chance to present your project. Fail to appeal to the right people, and all you'll be hearing are criticisms of skeptical people.

"Know your audience."

Dr. Bak Nguyen

When you were crafting your **WEBSITE** and your **PROMISE**, you were addressing the person with a problem. Usually, that same person is also the decision-maker of to buy or not to buy.

If you are talking to the right party, your sale may conclude. If not, you are merely wasting your time and money.

With the business plan, it is the same strategy. The people that will make the difference are the decision-makers. Appealing to them is your only concerns. Talk from the heart, entrepreneur to entrepreneur, financier to financier.

Your wording and numbers should always keep in mind that your audience is sharp and high informed. They will see the cracks and the flaws in your presentation, be ready to address their concerns.

If there are asking the question, rejoice since you have their attention. Now that you are in, make sure to keep their interest.

This is where the **NARRATIVE** will be of uttermost importance. Your **NARRATIVE** is mainly the story of how you plan to succeed to achieve your **NUMBERS**.

In other words, your **NARRATIVE** is the **PROMISE** you make to the financiers, bankers, and investor: how you will leverage on the market to create a profitable position.

HOW - HOW MUCH - HOW LONG

Make sure to stay short, concise, and straight to the point. Keep most of your justifications and explanations to answer their questions or in the annex, but the **NARRATIVE** section, stay **bold** and **on point**.

Answer the main interrogations before they raise the question: **HOW - HOW MUCH - HOW LONG**.

On that, I encourage you to include a graph at the end of your **NARRATIVE** section, one representing the rise of your joint enterprise since they will be joining you!

Now, if they are still reading, you have done an excellent job, you have successfully captivated their attention and interest. Now, they have questions.

You do not know to whom you are speaking. You hate the feeling, right? Make sure that they know to whom they are talking too.

The last section should be the presentation of the critical player in your team with a short resumé for each person. Doing so, you are giving to the **FINANCIERS** a good idea of to whom they will be speaking to and how to address their questions.

In short, the business plan has two main objectives:

- **to introduce a subject of discussion of interest**
- **to create an opportunity to address the decision-makers**

This is why you must always keep in mind that everything you are writing in the business plan is for the benefit of your audience. People like to see to whom they are speaking to.

Make sure to include a good picture of the members in question. Just like speed dating, your business plan is the speed dating profile to open a conversation. And please, do not forget to smile in your picture!

"Walk them through your plans,
but from their perspective."
Dr. Bak Nguyen

With this, your business plan is completed. Make sure to add your contact information.

The title of this book was not HOW TO WRITE A BUSINESS PLAN or only BUSINESS PLAN as it initially called. It is **HOW TO WRITE A SUCCESSFUL BUSINESS PLAN** which should reach its objectives:

- **to introduce a subject of discussion of interest**
- **to create an opportunity to address the decision-makers**

Take the time to prepare and to sort out your data and numbers. Have the right wording, and I assure you, you will have that chance to present your idea to the decision-makers.

Just like the show Dragon's Den, you will have a few minutes to convince them of the originality and profitability of your enterprise.

It is not about your feelings; it all about their feelings! This is why you should be the one drafting the process, at least for the first time. From the **WEBSITE** to the **NUMBERS** to the **BUSINESS PLAN**, you are the entrepreneur, the visionary.

They will want to hear it from your mouth, from your words.

Take this opportunity to prepare, to refine, and to polish your speech and presentation. Then, hire professionals to rewrite everything; what you hold in hand was merely a draft!

This is the **MILLION DOLLAR MINDSET.**

Dr. BAK NGUYEN

CHAPTER 5
"THE EXPERTS"
by Dr. BAK NGUYEN

Shocked? Now that you have done all the work, you need to hire someone, an expert to redo everything, spending money and time?! I used to share your exact feelings, but experience has taught me to let go and to do it the right way.

The main reason why you want someone else to work on your plan is that you'll need an exterior vision of your thoughts. Those experts will have to make sense of your ideas and visions. They will need to refine your words and your numbers until they can understand it.

If they can, so will the financiers, bankers, and investors. On top of it, they will be writing a business plan, one without pride. You need your business plan to look as neutral as possible. Optimistic, bold, but dull, to allow the reader to make up his/her own opinion of the proposal, not just selling them a dream.

The experts will also be able to complement your numbers and market views with market research and use numbers that they know the financiers will appreciate.

To each our craft and skills. Keep in mind that those you hire to write your business have written many business plans before and know their audience much better than you do. You might hold the message; they are masters in communication. So trust them.

That was for the wording. Of course, you might need an accounting firm to look at your numbers and projection. The name of the firm and those signing the numbers next to your name are also of prime importance.

Once you have the attention and interests of your investors, it is all about the **credibility**. If you have great name vouching for you, your credibility is going up. If you stand alone, be sure to be profoundly challenged.

Significant firms, great names, experts all bear the weight of their cost. On this, you can trust me. It might be hard at the beginning to afford the right people, but only with the right people, you may have a chance to present your proposal to the real decision-makers.

Once again, it goes back to your **NUMBERS** and **AMBITIONS**. If you are looking to reinvent the world, the cost of your business plan can largely be justified, and the final result will mainly make up for the initial investment.

Now, if your project was too small to bear such cost, my best advice is revisited your **NUMBERS** and **AMBITION**. The time you'll be spending will be the same, the energy you'll be deploying will be as high, why not make to worth your while?

You are asking people, financiers to believe in you and to take a leap of faith. That's insecurity, risk. Those people are advert to risk. The only way to offset the threats was to justify it with a profitable outcome, one too gib to be missed.

"It is too good to be true…" you might hear this one often. Trust me, the Financiers, the decision-makers, they are actively looking for those opportunities to address inefficiencies of the market. If you can illustrate your point of view and prove your **NARRATIVE**, you have just found your partners.

So if you will have to ultimately delegate the writing of a business plan to expert, why bother to start with? Because it is your business plan, not theirs. You need to be able to breathe and to feel that business plan inside out.

Remember, the business goal was to establish the opportunity of a dialogue between you and your financiers, the people with the means to make your company into a bluechip's success.

They have the money; you have to show them your potential. And no one will hear of your potential if no doors, rear doors open up to you.

That is why you will need a solid business plan, one written by experts leading their industries and proper names. I started this book from my experience as a veteran entrepreneur, one looking to move ahead as light as possible, as quickly as possible.

Today, I am working on the reengineering of my industry, dentistry, the odds are enormous, but so are the challenges too. I have a clear vision, but by myself, there is just so much I can do.

I have written myself the initial business plan, at the demand of my mentor Christian Trudeau, a man who built company in the billions.

I did so without too much resistance. I also built the website of Mdex and knew it content inside and out. The day I put the two together that day, I took to step forward.

The first one because I could make sense of my **NUMBERS** and **NARRATIVE**, with real numbers from the field.

The second step forward was somehow unexpected. By being open and welcoming the aid of the experts, I was able to evolve from there, to save them times since my logic served as a basis for their understanding.

I took the time to transfer to them my vision and passion. In return, they propelled the business plan to the next level, looking at angles that I never thought of.

I can tell you that today, I am so ready to face the questions and the challenges that I do not have to project anything anymore. I have been immersed in my **NARRATIVE, NUMBERS,** and **MARKET** for so long now that I now the wording, the inflection points and the right feelings to convey.

In other words, I am ready to meet with my future partners. With the means invested, I have succeeded to have qualified partners to help open the doors of the decision-makers. My mentor, Christian Trudeau, is leading the charge for the first round of financing of **Mdex & Co**.

His name alone opens doors. My job is to establish trust and to keep the conversation going, one that is worth the while of the decision-makers. I am working on a bluechip and a chance to change the world as we know it, from the dental perspective. I only could do so if I were ready and willing to keep evolving.

It took us nearly a year to refine and polish the business plan. For someone as impatient as I am, trust me, it took much to convince me of the validity of this process. Having done so, I can only tell you that resistance is futile unless you like to fail.

More than once, I have heard university professors saying that a business plan is useless. I used to agree with them. Today, I know how wrong the statement was. A business plan is not a plan, merely a process preparing you for what's coming.

You can improvise, but doing so, you won't be having many partners since they would understand what you are trying to do or how you are planning to do it.

Even if you are very well organized since on exterior eyes have sorted out your data and **NARRATIVE**, no financiers will take the time to sort out the information, they will move on to the next project.

That, I learned from Christian Trudeau, my mentor. The man spent decades modernizing the **Montreal Stocks Market**. He led the team who computerized all the transactions. By the end of the day, the wording is reduced to three letters and the numbers to a price and many ratios.

This how the decision-makers are used to read businesses. If you do not fall into those ratios, no matter the letters, you won't fall into their attention. That's the wisdom that I learned having the privilege to exchange with a mentor of the caliber of Mr. Trudeau.

To you, I can only show you what I am doing, how I came to that conclusion, and why. It is up to you to decide and to draft your destiny. I said draft since you will need time, expertise and help to write your final destination, your chance.

And where to look for those experts? Start with your accounting firm and ask questions. If there can point you in the right direction, you are in good hands. You have some references to go to.

If they are looking at you with aliens' eyes, maybe it is time for you to look for another firm, a bigger one. Business is all about connections and who you know. People of ambitions all know each other and know to whom to refer.

People with lesser ambition will hang around the crowd with the same aspirations and connections. So it is not how many people do you know, but the quality of the people you know and your relationship with them.

I took me years to finally accept you I was and my purpose in life. What I found out was to attract people to you instead of going to them.

For the last two years, I've been very bod and verbal about my views and my mission. That brought me much attention. People who do not know me well all thought that I was seeking care for my pride.

They couldn't be more wrong. I was setting the table for my business case and the presentation of my business plan.

For two years, I established my credibility as a visionary and a leader in my field. Most people (Financiers and potential partners) are still following me on social media. Even the decision-makers who I am meeting often heard of me for months by now.

I have a name, Dr. Bak. I have experts building a rock-solid business plan and ambitions to enlighten the room. I learned from the best mentors, Christian Trudeau, and Dr. Jean De Serres, and I have prepared for a long time:

"Today, I am secured enough to share, not to sell."
Dr. Bak Nguyen

This is my business case; this is my business plan. May it inspires you to reach out for the sky and to write your business plan, your draft to your destiny. Be bold and be open, write down your thoughts and welcome the help fo experts.

Don't be cheap, since you will need to be surrounded by people smarter than you are. However you valued your worth, the people you seek help from should stand way above you.

You might not have the means in the next time to pay them their worth, appeal to their ambitions and generosity by proving them your worth.

That was your first cornerstones. Them, evolve from their help and counsel to grow into the **NARRATIVE** you drafted. Now that you have delegated the writing part, you can now concentrate your effort in expanding into the person to shoulder and empower the **NARRATIVE** of your dream plan, your business plan.

This is the **MILLION DOLLAR MINDSET.**

Dr. BAK NGUYEN

CHAPTER 6
"THE COMMUNICATION"
by Dr. BAK NGUYEN

"At the end of the day, business is communication."
Dr. Bak Nguyen

I used to think that writing down my plan was a mistake. That anyone could then stole my idea and beat me at my own game. What a lack of confidence. How can someone beat at my own game? This would be an excess of faith leading to sure failure.

The truth is that business is communication, and anything of worth will require a team, counsellors and partners. No way to keep that secret if you want to grow. It is then that I came up with the following:

"Sharing is the way to grow."
Dr. Bak Nguyen

Not just in business, but also in Life with a capital L, sharing. Getting back to the subject at hand, you wrote a business plan to present and to share its content.

You are hoping for the attention and the interest of the decision-makers. You need them as much as they need you, the only difference is that right now, they have a choice, you might not.

That's why you need to stand out from the crowd of entrepreneurs seeking money and support. You are in seduction mode. You are there to seduce them with your plans to take over a market and to change the world. You are there to make them productive while they are looking from afar.

Do be mistaken, and you will be working for them, that what you asked for. In exchange, they might provide you with the means and the tools to realize your dream and vision.

"Without money, you will have a good idea. With the right funding, you have a shoot to change the world!"
Dr. Bak Nguyen

Forget your pride and insecurity; it is time to embrace your purpose and your destiny. Suit up, fuel your confidence with grace and share your message, your vision.

"The idea is just the beginning of the journey. The execution is the plat de resistance."

Dr. Bak Nguyen

The execution never forgets that. You had a genius idea, bravo. Now it is time to roll up your sleeves and to walk your talk. It is time for you to embrace the hope that you hold the solution and to work tirelessly until you are proven right.

That's inhumane and impossible to withhold for an extended period. This is why you will need a team, people complimenting you where you are weak or blindsided, and people relaying you as you run off of energy.

"It is not about you anymore; it never was.
It is about the idea and the solution."
Dr. Bak Nguyen

If you can understand that, you are ready to have a team; you are a team player. Only then, your partners will invest in you and with you.

You are asking them for a leap of faith; you too must leap, one where you are sharing your views and the merits. After all, you are asking them to share the risks.

I hope that it helps to put things in perspective, entrepreneur to entrepreneur. You must be ready to face the music and the dance before coming to the ballroom. Your business plan was your way to force an invitation.

Then, you will have the floor, a little while and only once. Either you talk your way in, showing them your worth and vision or you holdback and might never have the chance to show the world the potential you hold, hide inside.

It took me nearly 20 years to accept who I am and my calling. Now, I am all in, with some wisdom, but all in. This brings me to the beginning of this chapter: **"At the end of the day, business is communication."**

I said that in my first public conference at the **John Molson School of Business**, **Concordia University**. It came out on its own, and I just reacted to my own words. If one wants to be in business, one must master communication and the narrative at all time.

To charm and seduce your clientele, it is about communication: making them hear your promise and then, keeping your promise. To your client, you are promising to ease their pain or to make their lives better.

To your partners, employees, and investors, you are making the same kind of promise: to make their lives better, wealthier. That is the reason why they trust you invested in you.

As you can see, I added employees to the list. It is not a mistake. They are your workforce and your impact team. Without them, you do not have the strength to withhold the fort for too long. Appreciate them and make them feel like part of the adventure.

I know this book is about writing a successful business plan, but now that I have cracked the code wide open for you, I know that you will be in a position of power sooner or later.

This is why I take this opportunity as I still have your attention to remind you of your responsibility to your team and partners.

Respect them, share with them, and keep leading the way. Some will be with you only for a little while. Others will share a more significant part of the journey. To each their choice, you do not own them, nor do their own you.

"Share and make the most
of the present time…"
Dr. Bak Nguyen

And when it is time to say good, move on, keeping the excellent memory in mind. Welcome the newcomers, the adventure continues.

For your partners, it might be the same. Some will change their interests and their goal over time. Be respectful and do not hold back someone because you are holding to the past... it will never end well.

So business is about money, but not all of the journey is about money. It is one about choice and value; this is the soul of your enterprise.

For those of you that this subject appeal to, I wrote a book co-signed with my mentor, Christian Trudeau on the matter, my 35th, **HUMAN FACTOR**. I will invite you to have a look at it. **HUMAN FACTOR** is our take on management and Human Resources.

But this chapter was about communication? Communication, not marketing. All of what you just read is communication, the communication of a dream, a way to organize, a way to do things, a way to tackle a problem.

Shallow your pride and leave your insecurity, the idea was only the start. Share freely and boldly. Then, react to your words, the reactions you are receiving and the feelings, this is how you will evolve and grow from that initial idea.

So with the financiers, the banks and the investors, I have grown more and more friendly, sharing my vision with them. The more I share, the more they can grasp and feel my imagination.

As they see the vision and feel it, we now share a new reality, one in which they need me as much as I need them to make that reality a better future for all parties.

I have failed too many great ideas in the past to tell you otherwise. **"Alone one goes far, together, we go far."** In business, there is no better wisdom. You need a team, so learn to share and learn to communicate.

For that, you will need to feel secure about who you are and to welcome the diversity, the difference, and opposition. Leading does not mean to compromise, leading means to keep an open mind and to lead loyal to the goals; this time, the goals were yours.

Be genuine and people with trust you. Some won't, it is not of your concern, apply yourself to fulfill your promise to those following you.

This is not true when you are looking for clients, but for partners and investors too. A while ago, when I was building up **Mdex & Co** and starting to share my vision, looking for financing, I met with a young and beautiful banker, Rouba Sakr.

I showed her my vision and stayed genuine and loyal to it. She read everything, my words, my none verbal, my vibe, my numbers. When the numbers didn't make sense, she fought with me to have numbers that she could vouch for.

She believed in the project, and our loyalty was not to one another, but the realization of the vision. Months later, I even invited her to join me on stage at the **Olympic Stadium** in Montreal for an entrepreneurial keynote.

We shared our story, one that al entrepreneurs could relate too, one without numbers, but universal one: **trust** and **communication**.

Don't worry, I have invited Rouba Sakr to join this book, and the second part of this book will be her side of the story. You see, I am committed to sharing with you, not only my words and thoughts but also my experience and journey.

Except for the numbers and the other names than our own, we will disclose with you how to have a **SUCCESSFUL BUSINESS PLAN**, one that is changing the world as we speak. It was all communication.

"Be genuine, honest, and respectful.
Those are the basis of communication."
Dr. Bak Nguyen

Then who yourself and who you are talking to before engaging a dialogue. You will both gauge each other find a way to communicate.

When two parties come together there are only two options: either they start connecting, which in this case the energy will go up, or they start comparing, in which case the energy will spiral downward.

Keep that in mind and be open to share and look for a connection, not a comparison.

You are writing the world of tomorrow from your words and thoughts, choose your words carefully, and apply them with gentleness.

You are holding power to write the future, only if your master communication.

This is the **MILLION DOLLAR MINDSET.**

GIVE YOURSELF THE MEANS OF YOUR VISION,
THIS TIME, STAY IN THE BOX, MASTER THE BOX.

Dr. BAK NGUYEN

CHAPTER 7
"THE CLOSING"
by Dr. BAK NGUYEN

Even if the title of this chapter is **THE CLOSING**, we are far from the end, merely the end of the first steps of an exciting journey.

By now, you have a **WEBSITE**, the draft of a **BUSINESS PLAN** but moreover, you are trained to live, to feel to breathe your business plan.

I asked every one of you to roll up your sleeves and to do the work yourself, building and designing your **WEBSITE** to move on to write your **BUSINESS PLAN**. Then, I told you to hire professionals and expert to start over.

The final result should be stunning since you have sorted out and refined on the raw material (talent and ideas). The professionals with polish it and take care of the presentation.

Once again, do not try to do everything by yourself. Do not merely delegate either; you still need to pour in your soul to breathe life to the vision.

"Trust comes with familiarity."
Dr. Bak Nguyen

Is it okay if I ease your way in the next step, **THE CLOSING**? You know that all that you have achieved is leading you to this exact moment, one where you have the opportunity to present your ideas and plans to the decision-makers.

While it was all about them (the clients and the financiers), this stage is all about you! Yes, you, and not you that you think.

What you did in the past, your plans and ideas, all of that is part of the history, which has allowed to be there, in front of them. Now, they want to know the future, the future you!

If you can incorporate that fact in your mind, you will have score big time. **THEY WANT TO KNOW THE FUTURE YOU**, the one that will be stirring the enterprise to new heights. If you boil it down, it now all about how trustworthy you are.

They are investing big money into your company, they want to be reassured that you know where you are, but more importantly, that you know who you are! Because of that, they will be asking questions, many questions.

I can't tell you how to answer those questions, but here a tip that can be very useful: months before meeting with them, add them on business networks like LinkedIn. Some will welcome the connect; others won't. It does not matter much.

Then, start sharing your thoughts and want you are doing. Since you are sharing and not selling, you will I meet less resistance. Also, the exercise will help you be better and more comfortable delivering your core message.

No matter the numbers of views, keep doing that consistently. You'll be surprised by how many people in the right industry will have heard of you.

Since you are doing that with discipline and genuinely those people you are asking support from may have seen your face and message more than once by then.

You are familiar, your speech is not alien, and they might feel right at home even if you are meeting with them for the first time.

I learned that while I was defending my nomination as an **Ernst and Young Entrepreneur of the Year**. I didn't win the grand prize, but everyone knew who I was and wanted to know me better. Trust me, in business; you cannot ask for more!

"The message must be clear and bold, and always about them, not you. "
Dr. Bak Nguyen

So what's next? The closing argument, or if we want to be accurate, the opening of the real conversation. You have their attention, and now it is time to deliver, better, to over-deliver.

Just like a business card, your business plan is merely to put your foot at the door, those of the decision-makers.

The more precise your business will be, the more you are orientating the questions that you'll be receiving.

I told you to be bold, concise, and straight to the point. By being brave, you are provoking a reaction, by being brief, you are influencing the questioning, by being straight to the point, you are proving that you have a business mind.

Then, what you need to do is to listen and be receptive to the comments and the questions. Embrace whatever angle that you might be thrown at and in. Your security was that you know your market and business plan inside and out.

Now, the first thing that the financiers will do is to test you to throw you off base. The more they were impressed and loved you, the more they will test you.

This is a good sign, and it means that they have interests in your views. Now, they want to know if you are the right person to stir the boat.

Just like Christopher Columbus, who went to Queen Isabella, the Financiers might give you a command and a boat to stir. Be grateful and hopeful, be open to the questioning. I am leveraging much fun from experience.

I don't see it as a test nor a way for them to destroy my ideas; I see it as a game. Some times, when I am thrown a curveball, I stay calm, and if I do not have the immediate answer, I ask for a chance to come back to them.

And I do, a few hours, a day at the most later. Each time, I ask for their contact and reach for them.

You'll be surprised by the response. They love people keeping their words. What was supposed to be a test and maybe a trap, I leverage it into a chance to connect personally with the person.

I will also need to give satisfaction to the initial challenge… even if most of the time, there was no perfect answer. "Here is my take…"

Your words and your credibility, this is all that matters once you have passed the door. With experience, I have come to look actively for this kind of opportunity to prove myself, genuine and confident.

"Confidence does not mean to be full of yourself and to have all the right answers. Confident means to be secured enough to be open to listen and to discover new alternatives."
Dr. Bak Nguyen

That kind of attitude got me the respect and friendship of many decision-makers, all people that have titles longer than my name.

But at the end of the day, we are all people looking to connect, **genuinely** and when possible, **happily**.

To me, this is why I love what I am doing. Some people will see it as I spend my days begging for money. The way I see it is that I have the chance to meet with smarter people to test the idea. I will present myself at my best, serving with all of my power.

Some will return my ball, and we will start running. They will make me run out of my comfort zone, and so will I. I am a sport, and I welcome the challenge. You know what? So are most of the people I am meeting!

Respect and security, those are the keywords if you are looking for a favorable outcome. The more I am doing this, the better I get.

False! I keep coming back at the table, but with bigger and wilder projects, the person in front of me keep changing, and the game is never the same. The rules keep changing, and the only thing that remains is the sport and respect.

Be secure enough to welcome the challenge, walk your talk, and prove your point. Remember, **leadership is not compromising**; it is to make the thought call when needed and in line with the established goal. This is what the Financiers are trying to get out of you.

Thank them for their time and their interest. I have seen too many great minds lost their chance simply because they were not the sport type.

This is a game, a dangerous game of money and a way of life, the wind will change, and the sea will rarely be calmed, so find your fun riding the wave.

I find it easier to provoke the storm to ride instead of reacting to it. In financial term, fuel your ambitions. Aim for the moon so that the risks can be justified. You will never be able to secure anything at 100% unless you are a liar or inexperienced.

Perfection is not part of the equation; only your **attitude to react** will be the **STABLE VARIABLE**. You started this journey on an idea; this book has empowered you on the way to write a business plan, the next step is to throw away the project and to keep the skill and experience you've gained doing it.

In financial terms, this is called **financial wisdom**. We started this journey saying that it is not about you, but about them: your clients, then, the financiers.

But now that you have reached the other side of the door, it is all about you... I mean your attitude!

GENUINE, **CONFIDENCE**, and **RESPECTFUL**. You'll be surprised how the other party will react to you. If they love you, they will help you to succeed. I mean, you don't know what you don't know. What about if your numbers were wrong? Or your market, or your wording?

That would usually mean that you are out, and you've burned your chances, right? Not necessarily. If they felt the vibe and ambition, if they saw the vision and liked you, some times, they will help you fix what they know was wrong.

Money is cold and has no odor; not necessarily. In **part II** of this book, I will share with you the other side of the story, the perspective of a banker. One of my bankers has accepted to join this journey to help you understand the success behind the dance.

Rouba Sakr was the banker who was defending the **Mdex & Co** project. She was the main person that had to package the project into word and numbers the bank could accept. I promised her to let her the first take of this narrative so that I will refrain myself from any spoiler for now.

Just know that it is the first time that a banker will join in this kind of journey to give you the complete story, one with both sides.

The **Mdex's** story is a unique one, one that promises to change the world from the dentistry perspective. Going to the dentist will never be the same after **Mdex**.

The ambition is there, and the story you are reading is being written as we speak. All of the strategy and the steps explained in this book were steps that I took, as the founder of **Mdex** and an **Industries' Disruptor**.

You won't have to be as bold, and if it worked for me, it would serve you as well.

I am perfectly aware that most of the things that you read in this journey are not the classic **HOW TO WRITE A BUSINESS PLAN**.

I added **SUCCESSFUL** to the title, and that changed the course of the trip altogether. This is not an exercise; it is a testimony and the recipe leading to that success.

Do what I am telling you in here, step by step. I can guaranty that you will have a shot to speak in front of the decision-makers and that you will have refined your idea to a degree worth both your time and their.

For all you who thought that the business plan is dead and useless, sorry. I do understand your point of views, but from experience talking with the people from the other side of the table, a business plan was a most.

This way to write a **SUCCESSFUL** business plan is a reboot of the protocol, one that will be useful to the entrepreneur and relevant to the financial partners.

Am I convinced of my words? You bet. Going through the next part of this journey, you will better understand why I am that much convinced... I too had my share of failures.

I am still standing here showing how it is done because I am still embodying the hopes of an industry, even two industries (dental, finance) to be right and to successfully change the world.

Without further delay, here I rest my case and will open the stage for Rouba Sakr so she can tell you the rest of the story.

This is the **MILLION DOLLAR MINDSET.**

Dr. BAK NGUYEN

PART II

THE BANKER'S MINDSET

by ROUBA SAKR

introduction by
Dr. BAK NGUYEN

CHAPTER 8

"A PASSIONATE BANKER"

by Dr. BAK NGUYEN

With **HOW TO WRITE A SUCCESSFUL BUSINESS OOK IN 30 DAYS**, I shared with you what I would be teaching my son so he could build his own business and empire. I also find it of importance for you to have the point of view of the other party, the banks.

To give you a complete perspective, I have invited my former banker, now close friend, Rouba Sakr, to join us. My story with Rouba goes a long way.

Rouba is a young and attractive banker. That's the first impression she gave as she seduced you with her smile, kindness, and look.

After the introduction, she seems dedicated, kind, and passionate. To most people, that is a front, a public persona that we've trained ourselves to display in public.

Rouba, if you have the chance to get to know her, is that persona inside and out. She has no front; she is that genuine and passionate person you shook hands with.

But kindness doesn't mean weakness. Rouba has a sharp vision and kind words. A deadly mix if she is not on your side of the trade.

More than her beauty, I learned to know and respect her as a banker, but moreover, as a business person and as a friend.

If it wasn't for her dedication or, in my vocabulary, her stubbornness to see this project through (**Mdex & Co**), I might not be writing this story today. In short, the most ambitious project ever financed in the dental field has her handwriting all over it, literally.

For that, I am humbled and grateful that she believed in me... despite myself. I've promised Rouba to give you the details and her side of the story.

As the story unfolds, **Mdex & Co** is now in expansion, opening a second complex and well on the way to reshaped dentistry as we know it. For those of you with interest in **Mdex & Co**, I will invite you to read **CHANGING THE WORLD FROM A DENTAL CHAIR**, my 7th book.

After the ups and downs, we have come to respect the teacher other and are now good friends. She accepted my invitation to share her point of view of our journey... not often have a banker and an entrepreneur team up to deliver you the complete story.

"There are always two sides to every story."

This time, you will have the whole story. No numbers, names, or trade secret will be disclosed, but you will have the privilege to share her thought process and how a banker sees the world!

Even if I signed Rouba out of friendship, I truly believe the unique value that she is bringing to this endeavor and book.

Also, you will be reading about our "love and hate" story within the next chapters. I have promised Rouba that she will be the first one to tell her side of the story.

I am grateful to her to have not given up on me in my most desperate times. Use those words with a banker and, usually, you are cooked! With Rouba, that was the beginning of a long story and a few sleepless nights.

" Influence and relationship go a long way in business and life."

Dr. Bak Nguyen

If you want to change the world, you cannot do it alone, that's a hard truth. As your ledger grows heavier, you will need allies on the way.

Banks are your allies, if and only if, you can seduce them and convince them of your vision. Loyalty and transparency are qualities that most people look for within a friend.

With banks, that's the core of the relation: **trust** and **transparency**.

They have questions. You will have to strip down naked (financially), so they can examine and assert your worth and potential. That's just standard protocol, don't get upset nor take it personally.

You don't have to be perfect, just comprehensible to their eyes through the language of numbers. Yes, they talk with numbers instead of words. They speak with ratios.

They see risks and rewards but mainly, look to reduce their exposure of threats to the minimum, since they are the one taking most of the risks and not having all of the upsides when things turn out great.

"To be fair, we, entrepreneurs, have a better trade of that deal. Be aware, be grateful."
Dr. Bak Nguyen

As entrepreneurs, our job is to have the vision, seduce clients, and investors with words of passion and overdeliver. Yes, overdeliver.

I said seduce with the best intention and meaning of the word: put yourself on your best day and sale yourself with all of your heart and mind.

"Your best, but you, pure you!"
Dr. Bak Nguyen

To over promise and under deliver will be your worst trait and your last shot in this industry. So be bold, but be you, at your best.

No new enterprise is risk-free. No new endeavor is above the uncertainties and, at least some dangers. The greater the adventure, the greater the risks… even if the upsides are worth it.

In plain words, if a project has 70% of chance of success, which are high odds from the entrepreneur's perspective, to the banker's eye, that same project has a 30% chance of failure. Unacceptable! And the accountants will all concur.

As a visionary and an industries disruptor, my mission is to reform industry and establish a new benchmark, how do you do that without risks? In other words, how do you get financing from your banks? Start by creating a trustful relationship with your bankers first.

" Shoot for the moon, that's the best way to minimize the risk/reward ratio. "

Dr. Bak Nguyen

By shooting for the moon, your risks go up, but not as much as your reward. It is a simple math game, but to sale, it, be ready to gear up your strongest suit! And may I add, you will not be able to remove that suit anymore within, at least, a foreseeable future.

So choose your armor well and be prepared. Just like any romance story, we seduce with our suit but, by the end of the day, we still have to show confidence and beauty once naked.

That's precisely the dance and seduction game that you'll be entertaining with your banker. I was lucky enough that mine was also pretty!

" Loyalty and transparency, those are the qualities you need to show to seduce your bank."

Dr. Bak Nguyen

I will let Rouba tell you our *"romance"* together. I am sure that you will all fall in love with her, just like I had. Remember, there are always two sides to each story.

For an entrepreneur, the only side of the story that will matter is the banker's side, at least, if you are trying to be financed.

So we did spend half of this journey learning **HOW TO WRITE A SUCCESSFUL BUSINESS PLAN**, but to be successful, that plan has to be understandable and clear to your primary audience: bankers and investors.

Without further delay, it's my honor and privilege to introduce to you a passionate and dedicated banker, Rouba Sakr, a woman with a kind heart and the determination to empower the dreams of those she respects.

This is the **MILLION DOLLAR MINDSET.**

Dr. BAK NGUYEN

CHAPTER 9

"THE FIRST IMPRESSION"

by ROUBA SAKR

The first meeting I had with Dr. Bak was a unique experience. Since I work closely with health professionals, I was expecting an encounter just like the ones I'm used to, meeting with clients.

That is, discussing current projects that all health professionals have in common, such as buying a new clinic, or new equipment, or improving their premises, etc.

In short, the same standard projects I was used to dealing with. As you will see, that couldn't have been further from reality.

Our first meeting was supposed to take place at the Mdex clinic, but Dr. Bak ended up changing the location and suggested that it took place at his own house instead. That put me in an uncomfortable situation from the start! Why at his home?!

Fortunately, his wife Tranie Vo was present at the meeting too. That day, I was greeted warmly, in a very zen and peaceful environment, a good cup of green tea waiting for me on the table.

I was pleasantly surprised! I am used to meeting my clients in their dental chairs and workplace, between a filling and a root canal. You can easily imagine what kind of discussions those type of meetings leads to, basically just focused on immediate needs.

This meeting with Dr. Bak was beginning in a very different path and had nothing to do with my typical workdays. So I thought to myself:

"Finally a dentist who's calm and unstressed!"
Rouba Sakr

They invited me to sit in the living room, and we all introduced ourselves. We started getting to know each other; we talked about this and that, we smiled, we laughed.

As the conversation went on, utterly unrelated to dental projects or financial needs, I started wondering the point of my presence there, I decided to address the matter myself and asked Dr. Bak about his current and future endeavors.

I saw his eyes brighten. Sitting on the edge of his seat, he started telling me his story, and the story of **Mdex**.

He told me about his studies in dentistry, about his career path, and about what he accomplished until now to where he sees the profession going.

"Passion and devotion were palpable!"
Rouba Sakr

I had never seen someone that motivated and ambitious. His non-verbal language echoed this as well. Then, he moved on to speak about his future projects. At that moment, I saw the fireworks illuminating his eyes.

Wow!!! It was impressive to hear him talk, to feel the passion elevating him. I was taking notes as fast as I could, as all those ideas flew all over, one project after the next.

"Innovation, perseverance,
and ambition were tangible."
Rouba Sakr

And I thought I was going to have a regular business meeting! How wrong I was! Then, I realized that the man in front of me was not only a dentist but an entrepreneur, a man who has a business mindset at his core, a man who thrives on innovation and progress.

In short, I had in front of me a visionary. Yes, a visionary!

"Warmth and humanity first, then vision
and credentials."
Rouba Sakr

This is the **MILLION DOLLAR MINDSET.**

GIVE YOURSELF THE MEANS OF YOUR VISION,
THIS TIME, STAY IN THE BOX, MASTER THE BOX.

Dr. BAK NGUYEN

CHAPTER 10
"THE FIGHT AND THE MISTAKE"
by ROUBA SAKR

UNDERSTANDING DR. BAK'S VISION

I have worked with many entrepreneurs. I have to understand them, put myself in their shoes, and understand their challenges and reality. I am often stuck between my clients' ideas and the financial institution's parameters.

I have to make my clients understand that even if I'm the only banker talking with them and their only immediate contact, I am not alone.

Many people who constitute my team surrounds me. I stand as an actor in an environment where there are many supporting actors.

Their roles and functions are of prime importance when negotiating with the Bank. To talk to me is to speak to them. I cannot even start to explain to you how it was to go back and forth between them and Dr. Bak's crazy vision.

My job was to bridge and juggle between the ideas of a visionary such as Dr. Bak and to deliver them in realistic terms to the Bank. And so was the other way around too!

Try to deliver the financial institution's expectations and parameters to a visionary man who considers his project simple and easily achievable? Big mistake!!!

I had to carefully explain all the institution's parameters in a language that Dr. Bak could understand! And above all, without any financial jargon!

As a banker, I consider it very important to have clear and keen communication between the parties. I believed in his vision, and I was willing to defend it to my superiors and the leadership of the bank. But to do that, Dr. Bak will have to understand all the issues at stake and the unavoidable financial rules.

That was the real challenge for him and me.

PROJECT ANALYSIS

The analysis of the project of the scope of **Mdex & Co** took quite a few days of work, intense work and spreadsheet puzzling! My end goal was to present the project to the analysts of the banks and to sell them the vision through financial jargon and ratio.

Yes, you read right: to sell them! Just like what you see in the Dragon's Den show. For me to do that, I had to analyze the project carefully, to be able to demonstrate that it contained the as fewer risks as possible.

Furthermore, I had to link the project with tangible financial parameters. Dr. Bak did have visionary ideas, but I had to deliver them to the analysts so that they seemed clear and realistic. That was my challenge!

I was stuck between someone that was ready to take an insane amount of risks to build his ideal, and a conservative institution used to approve mostly normative projects! What do I do?

"I was stuck between repeating the past
and building a possible future."
Rouba Sakr

The complete analysis took three days from the moment I received all the necessary documents.

As I said earlier, I proceeded to the comprehensive analysis of the project to see how I could present it in order to demonstrate that it was feasible, both according to Dr. Bak's words as well as to the actual numbers contained in Dr. Bak's documents.

"I was stuck between repeating the past and building a possible future."
Rouba Sakr

The complete analysis took three days from the moment I received all the necessary documents.

As I said earlier, I proceeded to the comprehensive review of the project to see how I could present it to demonstrate that it was feasible, both according to Dr. Bak's words as well as to the actual numbers contained in Dr. Bak's documents.

"The job of a banker is to bridge the present to the future. It is just not possible when you are stuck in the past."
Rouba Sakr

Especially when it came to the projections, for me, the projections needed to be the accurate reflection of the project, to show that Dr. Bak's concept reflecting the average risk related to the dental industry.

That would make it a profitable project worthy of attention. I wasn't trying to sell any daydream to the analysts, but rather a safe and realistic plan, the Bank invested in it, big time.

THE OBSTACLES

I must admit that I encountered many obstacles and pitfalls working on the **Mdex**'s project. But, according to visionary entrepreneur Dr. Bak, there were none! His plan was perfect and easy to achieve!

Projections are critical to bankers. It's the only way to evaluate the viability of a future project. But for a project of the magnitude of **Mdex & Co**, I only received four pages of projections, written in *WORD*, without even a cover page!

As soon as I saw that, I knew it was going to be a long day: it was the « homemade » type of document, with no effort put on the presentation aspect! That was very unlike Dr. Bak's professionalism.

I started flipping through the pages, and wow! Inside, I found once again the innovation, the vision, the dream... but those of a man who believes that his project contains no risk whatsoever. Guess what I found?

I saw a sales gross that doubled every year during the three next years, not a single trace of a calculation of the new loan to be granted, no specification about the salaries of the ten dentists that were supposed to be in place in the first year, nor any detail on the number of employees.

On top of that, no written explanation from the accountant to help me understand the report. In short, four pages that were telling me that everything was fine, in an ideal world.

I thus took the initiative to speak to the accountant. I wanted to understand where those results were coming from and how he had analyzed the case. He didn't tell me much; he just said that he had based everything on the meetings he had with Dr. Bak.

That was all I had in hand, and to the accountant, those were their expected projections. Like not every dentist are equal, and not all bankers are same, not all accountants are equals.

In the dental field, there is an accountant specialized in to understand the projection and budgeting of the dentists. This accountant surely had no experience in that field.

After haven't received such answers, which I must admit weren't very convincing, I asked the accountant if he had experience with the dental field. He told me that accounting was accounting, no matter the industry.

Sure, he may be right: numbers are numbers, but some parameters are specific to each industry, which have to be taken into account.

Do you know how a dental clinic works? Do you know that there is a possibility of the moratorium, the possibility to postpone the payment of the principle for a period?

Do you know that dentists may work as a guest dentist and be paid with a percentage of the gross? In short, each field has its specificities. The roadblock was the man himself, the accountant that I was stuck with.

Usually, I can work around this kind of roadblock, but to justify the financing of a project of the scope of **Mdex & Co**, there was no way around it.

I called Dr. Bak to let him know that the projections had to be modified, redo from scratch. I answered me: « Rouba, you have no idea how profitable the project is! Tell the Bank not to worry. I have to hang up now; I have a meeting. »

I hung up thinking to myself: « He is immersed in his projects, but not in the numbers!»

To recap: there was the accountant telling me that the numbers were excellent, realistic and well thought, there was Dr. Bak telling me not to worry because everything was easily feasible.

On top of that, there was the owner of Dr. Bak's premises telling me that it was a fantastic project and that everyone was just waiting for me (the Bank) in order to be able to begin achieving it!

Yes, the landlord of the building and their leadership were all pressuring me for a positive outcome as soon as possible. And all of those people we are talking in the back channels to high ranking officers of the bank.

In other words, I was the critical element that could make or break the project! You have no idea of the kind of pressure I was under. I believed in this project, but not on paper; the paperwork was killing both the hope and the dream.

Many things didn't make sense, both according to my knowledge and my previous experience.

THE DRAGON'S DEN

After having studied the file carefully, I contacted the analysts who were going to evaluate the project. I gave them the data along with many written notes of mine.

I did not want to lose my credibility nor the one of my client; I wanted to make sure that the analysts understood that the project was feasible and that my client had a lot of experience in dentistry, but that he was misguided and poorly counselled in terms of accounting. All he needed was an accountant who was knowledgeable of the industry.

And so I submitted everything, hoping that my notes would be convincing enough. Furthermore, meanwhile, I spoke to my boss about the case, who in turn talked to his superior. In short, the whole Bank knew about **Mdex & Co**.

Dr. Bak had no idea of what was going on. He wasn't aware that there was a whole army behind me trying to obtain a favorable decision in conformity with the financial institution's parameters!

Two days later, I received a negative response from the analysts, asking the same questions that I had asked myself earlier. Despite my notes, the project seemed not realistic to them, or too good to be true.

I contacted the analysis department and told them I would find answers to all their questions. I asked for a special derogation.

I would ask my client to change his accountant for one that would be more knowledgeable of the health industry, and I would afterward ask the analysts to reconsider the case without prejudice, meaning without my client losing credibility to the eyes of the Bank, since he had clearly been victim of wrongful counselling.

Luckily, they accepted to review the case in the advent of new projections from another accountant. That did not mean they would approve it, but at least it gave me a significant leeway.

My next challenge was to convince Dr. Bak to change his accountant! Oh, my God...

This is the **MILLION DOLLAR MINDSET.**

Dr. BAK NGUYEN

CHAPTER 11
"THE SAVING"
by ROUBA SAKR

FINANCIAL EDUCATION
HELPING A VISIONARY ENTREPRENEUR TO UNDERSTAND THE FINANCIAL MINDSET

After my discussion with the analysts, I immediately contacted Dr. Bak. My goal was to make him understand that his project was excellent and that I firmly believed in it, but that unfortunately on paper the numbers did not reflect at all its viability.

Dr. Bak is a man of his words and a loyal man. When I did reach him, I got the feeling that I offended him. He seemed insulted, just as if I'd said that his project was no good.

He had no idea that I had been fighting for days for his dream to come true! I had to remind him that I had managed to have the analysts give him a second chance, which usually is unthinkable!

"The entrepreneurial mindset tends to make all objectives seem easily reachable."
Rouba Sakr

No matter the projections related to it. Thus, entrepreneurs often need to be trained on how their financial partner works: while many entrepreneurs may consider the Bank as a dream crusher, it should be seen as a critical partner for your enterprise, a partner as vital as your accountant or your lawyer.

It's true, some times we do not give you the answers you would like to hear; but we have the tools to guide you so that you finally get those right answers.

Furthermore, we also work with partners that can help you find adequate solutions. That's what I was trying to make Dr. Bak understand; that I was seeking to help him as best as I could to attain his goals.

His stubbornness and blind loyalty to his friend and accountant made my task extremely difficult! In short, after our conversation, he said he would call me back…

Three weeks went by, and I had no news. I was still waiting. The days were running by, and Dr. Bak was nowhere to be found. In my head, the project was dead. I was so disappointed.

I was disappointed that he never saw my efforts. Disappointed that he thought I was rather an obstacle to his ambitious and significant project. I believed in the man and his vision.

Three weeks later, I received a call from one of my colleagues from another commercial department. She talked to me about Dr. Bak and about his **Mdex**'s financial projections that made no sense. I have to admit that I was shocked and hurt!

Dr. Bak had gone to validate my statements and my analysis with another department of the bank, and I was not even aware of it! I felt betrayed!! It was disappointing to see that I had never managed to gain his trust after all the efforts I had put into his project.

But on another note, I also felt somewhat reassured because my colleague was sharing my views about Dr. Bak's projections and that she was reaching the same conclusions as I was somehow reinforcing my credibility...

Two weeks after that incident, I received an email from a very renowned accountant's office that was sending me projections for Dr. Bak's project, while I was sure that Dr. Bak had forgotten about me.

I went through the projections, and this time, I was relieved. They were finally accurate and reflecting the viability and feasibility of the **Mdex & Co**!

They were only predicting some hardships during the first year, but that was normal and acceptable, as for any startup project.

I through the business' projections a few times, and I immediately called the new accountant to confirm that the predictions were at the height of my expectations.

He admitted having seen the initial projections and also thought that it had been very senseless from the client's part to have done business with the previous accounting firm...

I called Dr. Bak to confirm that I had received the projections and immediately sent them to the analysts.

I swear, the following two days were the longest of my entire life! I was impatiently waiting for an answer from the analysis department.

According to me, the projections were rock solid. Two days later, I finally received a response.

While my heart was pounding out of my chest, I opened the client's file... and wow!!!! It was approved!! Yes, approved!!! With a few predictable conditions, but approved!

I was jumping of joy! I was honestly so proud of myself, and so eager to tell Dr. Bak about our victory, yes our success! When I did, he was very expressive! He was as happy and excited as I was.

A week later, I received an invitation from Dr. Bak for lunch alongside him and his wife, Mrs. Vo. But not in any restaurant. It was an invitation to the RITZ CALTON, the most refined hotel in Montreal! I can tell you that it deserves a try; it's magnificent!

In short, I accepted the invitation. I had no idea what the reason for this invitation was. So I showed up, and to my greatest surprise, before the service, right after we ordered our drinks, Dr. Bak apologized to me, sincerely and genuinely!

He admitted he was sorry to have acted the way he did. He added that he rarely apologized, but this is of those times that he had to admit his wrongs. After all, I had allowed him to achieve a dream that he had been nourishing for a long time.

I was very moved by his words, mainly because I wasn't expecting them… At the moment, I realized why I believed in him and fought for his dreams. It was about the warmth and the genuine humanity that he embodies. Of course, I didn't appreciate that he went behind my back, but he too was fighting for his dream.

But when I heard his apologies, everything made sense to me. The friendship, the trust, the loyalty and, above all, being able to admit and to fix a mistake.

That day, a real friendship started between Dr. Bak and me. A friend that I am glad to have, now that I saw how he is loyal and treating his friends.

"Honesty and Genuity or what will make people believe in you, especially if you are looking for a banker's help."
Rouba Sakr

This is the **MILLION DOLLAR MINDSET.**

Dr. BAK NGUYEN

CHAPTER 12
"BANKING AND MEDICINE"
by ROUBA SAKR

How a visit to the banker's office can be like a visit to the doctor.

I love the analogy between a visit a doctor's office and a meeting with your banker. You would be surprised at the many similarities! Dr. Bak is a dentist, and at our first visit to his office, he asked you to fill in a health questionnaire. Why do you think?

Because he needs to understand your health history to treat your teeth, he needs to be aware of your whole health condition, as it can also have an impact on your dental health and on the treatments that may be prescribed to you.

When you visit any physician, be it for the first time or for the X time, the consultation takes place in the same fashion. They will ask you questions about the context of your symptoms: since when, where exactly does it hurt, is there any fever, etc. And then, they will examine you.

Of course, the examination is oriented according to the current symptoms, but it still needs to contain routinely acts such as blood pressure measurement, weighting, heart auscultation, screenings… in short, the doctor always requires a complete health assessment, even if you only show up because of a sore throat.

The doctor then gives you his diagnosis on the cause of your problem, as well as advice on how to solve it, and often, although not necessarily, he will write you a prescription.

The appointment usually lasts between 15 minutes and half an hour, depending on the issue; but the first appointment will always take longer because the physician needs to draw a complete picture of your health antecedents (family antecedents, illnesses, etc.)

Financially speaking, it's the same process. Instead of talking about your health condition, we are talking about your financial health. Do not be surprised if you are asked many, many questions and are required to fill up many documents.

On that, some bankers are even kinder than your family doctor, since they will be assisting in filling your questionnaire.

Just like a physician does, bankers are merely trying to get a complete assessment of your condition before we go any further into your case.

And of course, just as personal and sensitive is the nature of the information, just like your medical information, your financial information is treated with the utmost confidentiality.

In the visionary's mind vs. on paper: improving the financial side

As a visionary, your idea is undoubtedly brilliant. But saying so is not enough! You also have to explain why your plan can be profitable, and mainly, how you are going to make into a success.

In short, you have to show to your banker and your bank that there is a business possibility in your project and that you have the required knowledge and skills to achieve it, to deliver.

For that matter, banks usually require a business plan, a risk evaluation, and a detailed statement of your financial antecedents. You need to convince your banker that investing in your business will be profitable:

"Thus, do take enough time to prepare a convincing proposal."
Rouba Sakr

Your bank will ask for an exhaustive risks assessment. Be ready to explain how you intend to overcome the obstacles that may threaten to undermine the success of your enterprise. Your bank will also need information about the financial antecedents of your business.

If you just launched your business and have no financial antecedents yet, the bank will most probably proceed to a verification of your personal credit history.

Thus be prepared to present your loan guaranties. Do you have a guarantor? Are there other investors in your project? These are vital questions you will need to answer.

If your loan application is rejected, ask your banker to review it with you so that you see the reasons for the refusal, and can be able to improve your presentation for your next loan application.

Trust me when I say that this is no bureaucracy, although all the paperwork may fill like it, this is about commitment and seeking to understand each party and to forecast a predictable and bight future.

In short, the entrepreneur and the banks have to work together and to develop a trustworthy relationship to become partners, business partners. That's what the bank is, a business partner.

With the bank's financial support, you will bring your vision to life and heights.

This is the **MILLION DOLLAR MINDSET.**

Dr. BAK NGUYEN

CHAPTER 13

"THE MORAL OF THE STORY"

by ROUBA SAKR

I often think back about my success story with Dr. Bak, and use it as a basis to explain to my clients the importance of working together as a team on their projects, and that the end goal of all my questions and all the documents I ask for are to facilitate my work as their spokesperson and representative of their dreams and ideas in the Dragon Den.

The Bank may employ me, but my job is to defend and materialize the entrepreneur's business case. You read right the entrepreneur's business case.

For that, I need a case to present. My job is also to minimize the risk of having them refused by the Bank.

Time is money and nobody, especially the business people like to waste time. On that, bankers and entrepreneurs are alike.

It will take preparation and time to,
in time, save time with the financial leverage
of the Bank.

Rouba Sakr

I'm sure that many of us bankers have at some point had a client just like Dr. Bak, and that many of you, readers, have had a moment in your life where you could relate to either him or me in this story.

I learned many things throughout this adventure. The biggest lesson was perseverance: when you believe in something, no matter what it is, you will come out of it as a winner as soon as you have put all the necessary efforts in your endeavor, no matter the outcome.

You are the artisans of your dreams, and you can all achieve such a beautiful story as Dr. Bak's.

As a banker, I get to be immersed in a diversity of projects, each one more inspiring than the other. Sometimes I must refuse some for specific reasons; sometimes I have to refer to another banker who might have a better understanding of that particular type of business.

In the end, we are all looking for a profitable and positive outcome.

In those cases that I have the solution and the expertise to bring the project forward, I am, just like in the **Mdex's** project.

When I don't... I am just like a doctor who cannot right away promise recovery but who is ready to do all he can to improve the quality of life of his patients.

Some recover fully, some obtain a healthier quality of life, it's the same thing in the banking world: I can make your project come true at 100%, or help you achieve parts of it at first, or maybe delay your project a little bit so that it meets critical elements that you hadn't consider yet, or I can simply guide you towards someone who can help you where I can't.

But the important thing is, to be honest, and transparent. I know that I will always be open and try my best. Thus it should be the same for you.

You, entrepreneurs, are all so inspiring in your way; remember to be open to your bankers' advice, and to acknowledge their efforts to bring your projects forward. It is first and foremost a relationship.

All of you entrepreneurs are unique, and each of your dreams is different; every project I work on is a universe on its own. Each one of them helps me grow, day after day.

Thanks to all of you, by coming to me, you make me part of your journey of your dreams. And I want to be part of those dreams, and contribute to make them a reality and a success.

This is the **MILLION DOLLAR MINDSET.**

Dr. BAK NGUYEN

PART III
THE RISE
by Dr. BAK NGUYEN

CHAPTER 14

MDEX & CO
FROM CHANGING THE WORLD FROM A DENTAL CHAIR

by Dr. BAK NGUYEN

Now you have the complete story. Not yet, may I add, I have invited Rouba to join me on stage at the Olympic Stadium, talking to a crowd of entrepreneurs.

We went basically through the same story, not in-depth as in this book, but the deep enough to understand the relationship between a banker and an entrepreneur.

I apologized in public, and that was the main comic relief of the event. It was funny and genuine. Rouba's bank invested millions in **Mdex & Co**.

After that evening at the Olympic Stadium, I met with other bankers who were inspired by the kind of relationship that Rouba and I shared.

Fast forward in time, those among the new bankers I met that evening, one has come through for the next round of financing of **Mdex & Co**, where Rouba couldn't help.

I am happy to share with you that by the time of this writing more millions are invested in **Mdex & Co**, and if it wasn't from that good talk where I explained on stage the role of a banker to an entrepreneur, I might never have met with my future banker.

In a few weeks, we are opening a new complex **Mdex**, taking on the next phase of expansion thanks to the funds from the next round of financing.

I have to add, Rouba wasn't the same banker involved in the negotiations. A good friend of mine, a high officer of the bank who started as a patient a few years ago, put all of his credibility on the line to vouch for me and **Mdex & Co**: Anthony Siggia.

Without him and Rouba's determination, **Mdex & Co** may never have been financed. So what is the moral of the story?

BE BOLD, **BE GENUINE**, and **BE RESPECTFUL**. And then, deliver! This is how I managed to forge trust and friendship with each of my bankers; today, people I call my friends.

Where my business plan was flawed, they help me to address it, not because we were friends, but because they believed in the project. I had to do my part too, to listen.

Where my plan showed weaknesses, they helped me find a solution. With that, I over-delivered and kept them posted about the progress on the field.

This is the kind of relations that you need to build with your financiers, one of trust, and friendship. Money is still money at the end of the day, but with friends and allies, people are actively working to see you succeed!

Make sure to remember you helped you on your way up!

That being said, I will continue the journey with part III, borrowing from my other books to allow you a better understanding of who I am, what I am trying to do, and a sneak peek into the different fields of business.

WHAT IS MDEX & CO?
FROM CHANGING THE WORLD FROM A DENTAL CHAIR
CHAPTER 1
by Dr. BAK NGUYEN

The best advice I have ever received in business was not from a person but from the market itself! If you know that you are an entrepreneur, do not doubt yourself and never ask people what they think about your idea.

Please, allow me to explain: if what you are trying to do is new, nobody knows anything about it. Until it is materialized and well proven, it's just air, thin air that you have to believe in until it's done!

That's why we are called visionaries because we see and believe in things that do not exist yet.!

Even if we have the privilege and luck to have a mentor, never ask your mentor for his opinion about your idea. Instead, ask your mentor, even if he disagrees with the design, how he would execute it?

If there is any wisdom in my words, this is it! Trust in your idea and have the humility to learn from the rest of the world how to increment it.

Do you not have an idea? No problem, sit with a crowd, any crowd and start listening. You'll be amazed how people share as you demonstrate an interest in them and their problems. Yes, their problems!

As people open up to you, and many are sharing the same problems, you just have identified a niche, a market! Again, do not ask for opinions, ask for directions: what's wrong? How can I help?

If an idea comes to your mind after that, test it, ask the same people how they would react with this idea?

Do not listen only to their words: look at their body language to measure your impact as a whole. If you feel the excitement, the hope and if they use few words, you just found a sure winner.

On the other hand, if they use many, but many words to say that they like your idea and wish you luck, you haven't hit a major chord yet. If they stay silent, move on to the next idea.

It sounds like it made much sense, no? I didn't learn this from books, nor in a classroom, I got it from surviving in the entrepreneurial field, in the real world.

"Read people, read the crowd, and then you may have a chance in this game of entrepreneurship."
Dr. Bak Nguyen

Nobody is perfect, as much as no plans are complete. Things we read from history books are made perfect in the narrative. Perfection is a lie if you ask me!

Why? Because everything that we are is a response to Live, and since Life is always changing, no answer is neither perfect nor complete.

Even if it were perfect, by the time we put it on paper, it would have already started to become outdated. You have to look at marketing since the emergence of social media.

" Life is dynamic, and it is a permanent state of reorganization. So is the market."
Dr. Bak Nguyen

But the people, the crowd, most of them have been programmed to react in specific ways. That, you can foresee and have, at least for a short time, the exact response to.

In short, an entrepreneur will need many strengths to succeed in the market. The biggest one is recognizing his flaws and not making a handicap out of them. And then, he has to learn to read and connect with people and the crowd.

I have made it this far thanks to my imagination and my stubbornness to accomplish what I had in mind. But since, I have learned to master my reading skills and to recognize my flaws.

Since things have been much more comfortable; I move with more confidence, meet less resistance and rise way above my previous horizon.

" Before, they called me crazy. Today, they are eager to know more!"

Dr. Bak Nguyen

On stage, I love to finish my introduction with this phrase: « if I have changed the world from a dental chair, you are all in a better position than I am to change the world! » I do believe in every single one of those words.

In a dental chair, no one is in a sufficiently comfortable state of mind to open up and start taking the risk to embrace an opportunity other than to get out of the dental chair!

That was an easy read! I had to do something about it, and people started listening. That's how

I started my career as a visionary. It wasn't about business, and it was about being useful and friendly.

The only way to be that confident, and still have a love of the people is to serve them with all of our beings. Think about that: would you trust a dentist that has doubts?

Would you trust a surgeon that raises more questions than he presents solutions? Those answers are easy, but we often still fail to learn from them.

" Make it about them, always!"
Dr. Bak Nguyen

Mdex has three different branches:

Mdex & Co: the «hotel» concept that allows any dentist to own a micro-enterprise within the organization of a corporation.

Mdex Industries: the engineering company is revolutionizing how dental clinics are built, leaving no imprint on the building or next to nothing, while reducing the impact on the environment by almost 70% since most of our installations and divisions can be packed and moved to another location.

Mdex V: the "dental OS" that responds to the needs of dentists, to manage their clinic from a smartphone. **Mdex V** has also been optimized to remove as many filters as possible between the patient and his dentist.

At its core, **Mdex V** is the answer to the shortage of labor in developed countries since it will update the whole industry to today's communication technologies, reducing the need for manual and unnecessary phone calls.

Each of these branches has their creative spark.

Mdex & Co

The creative spark behind **Mdex & Co** is mainly a giving back feeling I had about three years ago: I was talking to an intern at **Mdex**, in her first year in dental school.

She mentioned how great this profession is to her and how it was inflicted with such strangely high rates of depression and suicide.

I jumped out of my chair! That was exactly what my dean, Dr. Jean Turgeon said to us when we were greeted in dental school, twenty-some years ago... and he was greeted with the same words at his first day in too. And today, we are still welcoming students the same way?!

If my maths are accurate, that meant that for eighty-some years, we are stuck with the same problem in the industry and we had ignored it, until it catches up with us.

That was simply unacceptable. In the field, there were less than five studies on the matter dated from the eighties and no real solution. I looked in the mirror: I did not see any signs of depression, even if I wasn't practicing my dream profession.

So I decided to roll up my sleeves and put on paper what kind of tools and environment I would have loved to have at my disposal to ensure my happiness and fulfillment as a dentist.

We started drafting up the **Mdex & Co** project: aiming to provide dentists with a chance to avoid the traps of the profession.

Things became interesting when I talked to a great friend and patient, Anthony Siggia, who loved the idea. He would later vouch financially for the potential of **Mdex & Co**. Let's rephrase that: the most ambitious project ever financed in dentistry has been vouched by a patient.

Today we are bros, and it all started on the dental chair. Relationships can go a long way at **Mdex**. From those sparks, **Mdex & Co** was born!

Mdex Industries

With **Mdex Industries**, I had no ambition to recreate the dental engineering, nor did I know I had the knowledge to do so. Here is how it started.

About five years ago, the Vice-President of the company owning the Scotia Tower, Mr. Serge Jodoin, offered me the opportunity to build a dental clinic at the 26th floor of that prime real estate building in the heart of the Golden Square Mile in Montreal.

It's not just the prestige; the view was amazing! I was in love the minute I entered the premises. He only had one main concern: was there any way that I could build without drilling that many holes in his building?

I had no idea, but I didn't want to lose the opportunity of that view, and I said that I would look into it.

To make matters worse, insurance companies were asking for crazy premiums, out of this world bonuses, to ensure the clinic since they would have to cover the liability of the 25 floors below us if any water leak happened. Two major roadblocks, but I refused to step down.

I thus had to find a way to bypass the typically required drilling when building a dental clinic. By chance, I had extra equipment left from the moving of my first clinic and a big basement at home.

I hired a small team and got close with the president of a small dental company, Mathieu St-Pierre. Together, we would find a solution.

The reality was that they were all looking at me as if I was crazy, but since I'm a cool guy and I was paying, they just did it!

And finally, it worked! At least engineering-wise! In my basement! Today, Mathieu and I are good friends, and we promise the world that this is just the beginning of our creativity.

With the time and money invested in that project, I had to tell my wife that I would be seeing patients at home... I never did. It took about a year to fix all our engineering concerns.

Then, I went back to the negotiating table; I even invited the VP to come and see for himself. He was blown out of the water, and we made it work: a dental clinic without the need to drill, without the use of copper eliminating the fire hazard related to the repairs, and with the possibility of a smart water leak detection system.

What he saw was a marvel piece of engineering. In his career as a landlord, he met with many people, but never had he encountered someone like me! But the 26th floor was long gone... He offered me other alternatives.

Today, **Mdex & Co** occupies two floors of that same prime real estate building. We passed the construction board, we obtained all our permits, and mainly, we built it!

The **NARRATIVE** coming with it is also one of the key appeals of our vision: we've managed to revolutionize the design of the dental industry.

We have reduced our imprint on the building to next to zero, we have drilled one single extra hole in addition to the main drain for the installation of ten operation rooms.

And we have also built respectfully to the environment: about 70% of our construction can and will be recycled as we will need to move, reducing our imprint drastically on the environment.

In short, because I listened, because I was in love because I didn't say no, it happened! Not overnight, but it happened.

From being a side project, today **Mdex Industries** has a bright future. From our projections, it might be the main cash cow to the Mdex group for a while! Patents are pending...

Mdex V

The creative spark behind **Mdex V** is a whole different story. As we were changing the business model of dentists and building a « hub » of dentists to replace the typical « lordship » model, most of the available CRM and managing software were just not adapted anymore.

Servers based and running on Windows 2000 priced at a few grants per license without any up to date communication tools such as email, SMS, cloud, sync... I couldn't simple buy those anymore.

So I sat down and started drafting what I would like to have as a dentist to feel empowered and proud of my position as an owner. "What do I own?" I wanted to know and hold it in my hands, at all times!

That's what I did: **Mdex V** is the way for any dentist to keep his entire practice in the palm of their hands.

The dentist can see at any given time, his patients and their contacts, his schedule, and his staff. Running a micro-business at **Mdex** is like playing a game on the smartphone, or as close as it could get.

We worked pretty hard to remove as many filters as possible between the patient and the dentist to humanize the relationship. **Mdex V** will serve as the best communication tool between the dentist and his patient without sharing private numbers.

Mdex V is also updating communication to the current century's trend, allowing patients to book their appointments online, modify them, and confirm them automatically by email and SMS.

This will avoid many phone calls from the secretaries, based on last century's protocol.

With the current shortage of labor, **Mdex V** is the particular jewel that will allow for cutting labor costs and solving labor issues, while bringing closer the dentist, his staff and his patients.

Within **Mdex V**, we did not forget about the patient either. The patient can opt-in to a download allowing him to access his x-rays, dental billings, and invoices for taxes and insurances purposes.

The patient will own and access his personal information from the tip of his fingers.

I often say that sharing is the way to grow. I will walk my talk. **Mdex** will be sharing its special jewel with the whole industry for a fraction of the cost of conventional and outdated means.

The **Mdex group** is many things, but all share the same DNA: serving the industry by empowering its users. Fundamentally, the creative spark came from listening and reading the industry.

If any, the main entrepreneurial traits coming out of this are **Humility** and **Confidence**! Humility to **listen** and **serve**, and the confidence to **execute**!

Make it happen. This is the **MILLION DOLLAR MINDSET.**

Dr. BAK NGUYEN

CHAPTER 15
THE NEED AND MARKET
FROM PROFESSION HEATH
by Dr. BAK NGUYEN

We often talked about understanding your market inside and out. I spent 20 years plus in a profession where I wasn't happy.

I wasn't satisfied because it wasn't my calling. I became a doctor to please my parent and the void we had as immigrants to be successful.

It took me 20 years to finally make peace with my nature and calling. The curious fact is that now, I am a successful dental cosmetic surgeon, one that people love and refer to. On top of that, I show no sign of neither depression or unhappiness.

Twenty years taught me to cope differently with my profession and my duties. But do you know that dentistry, as an industry, faces the highest rate of depression and suicide, for the last 100 years?

That was how I got welcomed into the profession by my dean, who got the same welcome by his dean. I felt down my chair when I learned that today, we are still greeting our newcomers with the same lines.

Having spent 20 years plus in this profession, I know the business inside and out. Not being in love with the job allowed me to identify what was broken and what needed to be addressed. This is how I survived my years as a dentist... and I am still practicing today.

But if I add my story to the ones of my colleagues who chose this profession without exterior pressure, we arrive with many similarities.

Within the next lines, I will share with you how I identify the needs of an entire industry and how I start connecting with my targeted audience.

This should give you a pretty good example of how to identify a need and to target a specific market.

TO KNOW AND TO UNDERSTAND A MARKET?

FROM PROFESSION HEALTH
Acknowledgment
by Dr. BAK NGUYEN

I've spent more than 20 years in the fields of dentistry from my first day in dental school. Like any other profession, our profession has its challenges. But is it right that we are facing one of the highest depression and suicide rates?

That's how I was greeted on my first day in dental school, with a warning. Then, the dean,

Dr. Jean Turgeon, told us that he was greeted with the same words as he first started in the profession too.

It was an anecdote that I soon forgot, until the day that I have an interesting discussion with an intern at **Mdex**: today, and we are still greeting our new students with the same words!

Something is wrong here, and numbers don't lie! I scratched my head, and I went digging around: even if dentistry is on top of the list of depression and suicide, many more health professions are getting close. And with the years, the numbers are just getting worse!

This is a matter of national health; we must act to protect those who are dedicating their lives in the service of others.

We are white coats; we are the healing hands of the planet. We must accept that we too need help.

I am starting in here a dialogue to start raising the right questions. To address a problem, we must accept the challenge, identify it and then, begin to find a solution.

This is it, the beginning of the acceptation and the diagnostic process. Is this book worth your time, white coats? Science and medicine are composed of three steps:

1- Diagnosis or Hypothesis

2- Treatment plan or Experiment

3- Reevaluation

It takes all three steps to succeed and to learn. But in medicine, we are dealing with lives, with people. We do not have the luxury of error, thank God.

So we are very well trained to go through the first two steps, but as we reached the third one, **REEVALUATION**, it is given to our peers in the form of a trial.

The scientific chain is broken. I do understand why the third step has to be overseen by peers, but we never thought of finding something to cope with the void, systematically!

Do I have your attention yet?

My brothers and sister in arms, dear white coats, we are all in this together. Together we will find a solution. It starts will opening up to share.

White coats, I salute you!

This is the **MILLION DOLLAR MINDSET.**

GIVE YOURSELF THE MEANS OF YOUR VISION.
THIS TIME , STAY IN THE BOX. MASTER THE BOX.

Dr. BAK NGUYEN

CHAPTER 16

ORGANIZATIONAL MATRIX
FROM HUMAN FACTOR

by Dr. BAK NGUYEN
& CHRISTIAN TRUDEAU

Since we are in the **"EXERCISES and EXAMPLES"** section of this book, I will share with you how writing a business plan will lead you to the actual building of a company, in this case, a projected bluechip.

The next chapter is a chapter borrowed from **HUMAN FACTOR** written with my mentor, Mr. CHRISTIAN TRUDEAU. Mr. TRUDEAU has many credentials under his belt.

He was Senior Vice-President of the **TSX, Montreal Stock Exchange** where he led the modernization of the Montreal Stock Market, bringing the power of computers and network on the trading floor.

I was CEO and FOUNDER of **BELL EMERGIS**, a division of **BELL CANADA** that was evaluated at 18 billion at the peak of the stock market. Mr. Trudeau built the company from the ground up.

Mr. Trudeau sits on many boards of directors while he keeps accumulating the president titles. He was president of **TRANSCONTINENTAL INTERACTIF**, **CENTRIA COMMERCE**, **AIRMEDIC**.

Today, Mr. Trudeau is the president of **OPTIMISTA**, a firm that he founded to accompany visionaries entrepreneurs to be funded and to revolutionize the world.

18 billion, that tremendous! Usually, this is the kind of story that we read in books. This time, Mr. Trudeau with whom I have developed a friendship, has accepted to become my mentor.

We wrote **HUMAN FACTOR** together as he was teaching me on how to structure and build **Mdex & Co**.

Mr. Trudeau is also leading the initial funding of the **Mdex Group**. While he is optimistic about the outcome, he is thinking ahead, preparing me for what will follow next, the **CORPORATION**.

To manage a team is one thing, to hire and manage 3000 employees spread internationally is another story.

I found of particular interest to share a chapter of **HUMAN FACTOR** with you, since you too, will be facing this step soon. More than the business plan or its execution, this is a journey, one that you might need help in.

Find a mentor, one with more wisdom and experience than you and be open to reinventing yourself. This will take much courage and confidence from your part to open up and change, not just grow, change.

Only from a mentor, one can cheat the timeline and the fatal mistake on his/her path. To build a corporation is undoubtedly an adventure and a challenge on its own.

To find your identity and to evolve another one, even greater. Does it have to be as hard?

Find a mentor, and you will start a dialogue that will ease your evolution; not your walk, your growth. In other words, your resistance to what is to come.

I am fortunate to have met many great people in my journey. This is part of the on-going dialogue that I share with my great friend and mentor, Christian Trudeau.

The business plan was step one. A successful business plan will lead you to a great journey. This is what await you ahead! Enjoy!

Without further wait, this how-to translate a successful business plan into a company!

ORGANIZATIONAL MATRIX
FROM HUMAN FACTOR
CHAPTER 6
interview of CHRISTIAN TRUDEAU
written by Dr. BAK NGUYEN

From the beginning of my career, I always said that to succeed, one needs a good plan. One that is clear to understand the steps without having to readjust at every step of the way.

Of course, you will still have to adapt, but the more precise and clear was the plan, the less one will have to adjust it.

When your goals are well defined, the next step is to break down your goals into steps and expertise.

"From a list of words, leaders will have to raise a team."
Christian Trudeau

That first team won't be the description of the structure of the whole enterprise, but it will serve as the skeleton of the different functions of the enterprise.

The difference is that the structure can and will change; it is the meat around the bone while the frame will remain.

In other words, the mission of an enterprise, its primary market, its philosophy may evolve, but they won't change. What might be changing are the products and solutions proposed.

"To think big and to clarify our goals will start a great adventure."
Christian Trudeau

From my experience, one will define the ambitions and the goals from day one, even before he/she has found his/her company.

Of course, things can change, they always do, but a leader does not change nor adapt his/her ambition as he/she goes.

A leader will leverage everything thrown at him/her to move closer to his/her ambition and goals. This is the only way to gain in speed and size.

That's why a leader will need a plan, a strategical plan. With a well-defined strategy and an excellent management team, this is how a leader will be able to concentrate his effort growing the business and the team, with more partners and clients.

Nobody will ever trust you, leave alone invest in your company if you are unable to show a clear vision of your company in less than 10 minutes. From my experience, people believe what they can touch and what they can see, not what they hear.

"A visionary needs more the open his mind to reach his ambitions more than he needs the means to do so. And trust me, means are key factors."
Christian Trudeau

The ambition is there, and it is the job of the leader to make it grow. With well-defined goals, a company chart will help to translate the goals into a master plan, a strategical plan.

This may be building on paper, and it will allow the expansion of the project and the elaboration of a team or teams to reach the goals.

You now have a team and a business plan. Those are what your investors will be looking at. With an idea, a good plan, you are increasing by much your chance to receive funding from the right people. With a budget, a timetable you can now start to recruit and to build your team.

"Without a plan, it is tough to advance,
not impossible, but challenging.
Did you need the extra challenge?"
Christian Trudeau

When I first started at **Bell Canada,** I was standing alone in front of the board of directors talking about a division that will be the number one in the field of electronic payment. And the internet has started yet…

I was standing alone, and all I had was my vision and my credibility, my experience, and my skill to organize. Within a few years, **BCE Emergis** was the third player in the field in North America with more than 3000 employees and 800 million in gross.

The ambition was there from the foundation. My organization has adapted with the growth, but the main components were as planned from the **ORGANIZATIONAL MATRIX**, the initial plan. It is me who had to evolve to fit my ambitions and success.

Because I believed, I worked countless hours to draft a vision that the board of directors could understand and grasp my concept and ambition. I was passionate and respectful. I was also knowledgable.

Because I was **knowledgable**, **committed**, and **respectful**, they trusted me and gave me the means to build a team and to reach the goals, one after the next.

Just like playing a video game, each time that we reached a goal, we had more resources to keep pushing for the next stage. Stage after stage, I sold the company to reach **18 billion** in market cap!

In between the victories and the steps, I kept a tight ledger to keep to the board of directors of the progress and the process on the ground. This is how they could follow the progression of the **STRATEGICAL PLAN** and gave me more resources to keep pushing.

Later, when shares of **BCE Emergis** traded in the stock market, my team and I was forced to comply to even tighter rules and report, not just to my board of directors, but also to the investors.

The **ORGANIZATIONAL MATRIX** allowed a baseline for everyone to follow the progress of the company, even the growth was still on paper and the wins, about to be signed.

Until it is done, it is air, just air. That air, put in perspective allowed the others to believe and to join me.

The more my structure was defined, the more solid it was to build on the ground, my ground. It is always easier to score on your turf. Well, with an **ORGANIZATIONAL MATRIX** in place, I could make every field into my turf!

On my turf, I like to share my confidence and my victories with my partners and teammates. I welcome the questions and challenges.

I love to have people laughing in my executive meetings, and this is how I can share the sensation of victory and satisfaction from the field. Doing so, I do not need to convince the board anymore; they have felt it themselves.

If they're looking for reports and ratios, those are all up to date and precise in files that I gave them before the meetings. I always like to be ahead of the questions.

Doing so, they loved me and reinforced the trust they gave me. This is all thanks to my **ORGANIZATIONAL MATRIX**, the master plan.

When I was senior Vice-President at the **TSX** (Montreal Stocks Exchange), I had no choice but to know my cases inside and out. I was in charge of computerizing the trades, so I had to understand the logic, the companies, and all the tools available for the investors to trade.

What I learned is that a company, no matter it field and size, got to summarized into three letters for identification and many ratios. This is how I cracked open the code of the financial market: three letters and proportions.

"Fewer words and ratios more than numbers."
Christian Trudeau

With experience and some initiative, I learned to tweak the parameters to have better ratios. This is how I came up with the **ORGANIZATIONAL MATRIX**: the art of converting rates and numbers into a team, with real people.

ORGANIZATIONAL
MATRIX

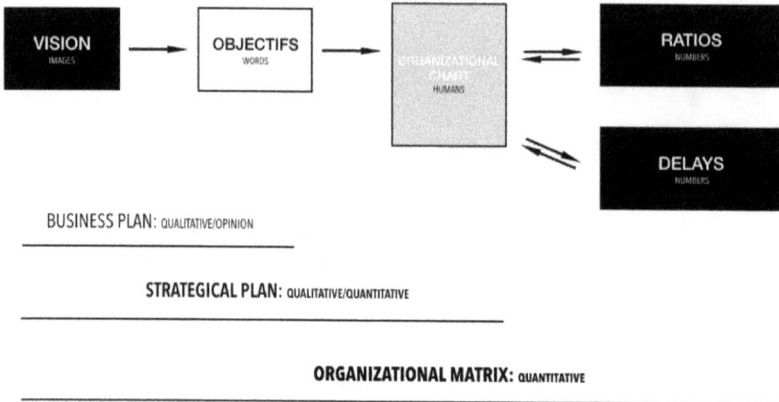

VISION
IMAGES

OBJECTIFS
WORDS

ORGANIZATIONAL
CHART
HUMANS

RATIOS
NUMBERS

DELAYS
NUMBERS

BUSINESS PLAN: QUALITATIVE/OPINION

STRATEGICAL PLAN: QUALITATIVE/QUANTITATIVE

ORGANIZATIONAL MATRIX: QUANTITATIVE

This graph will give you a sense of how the **ORGANIZATIONAL MATRIX** is built. First, you have to breakdown a vision into a list of goals are defined as possible; the brighter, the better.

Then, you convert those goals into a task that you associate with a person or a team of people. From the side, you then accumulate all the achieve goals to you add up into those ratios.

And this is how the board of directors and the investors will have a clear sense of what is going on the ground, with the perspective of the whole vision.

I have to admit that I am always surprised when I meet with smart and hardworking entrepreneurs, all very passionate who won't stop in front of anything but lack a strategical plan and an organization.

More than often, they have a basic business plan out of date and incomplete describing less than 50% of their vision. And why is that? Because they are fearful of having their ideas stolen.

"Fear won't help you if you are creating
an organization."
Christian Trudeau

As an entrepreneur and a leader, there are no half measures, either you are confident and trust in you and your ideas, either you will hide and see the opportunity passes you by.

Trust me, even if we all like to read that to be reasonable and to find the middle ground is a good thing, in business, there are losers and winners, and no middle ground in between. If you are not winning…

It is hard enough to succeed with a good business plan and resources, and I can't imagine how one will be thriving with half a project and even fewer resources… and without any confidence.

In business, to win, you have to take a stand and to defend it. Yes, people will judge you on what you said and did. That is part of the game. So if I know that I am being judged, I prefer to define the basis and metric on which I will be judged on: my organization, my team, and my ratios.

As for me, I do not judge; I help. Those entrepreneurs didn't have the experience or the formation to build and run a company. They need some support and to be stirred in the right direction to learn to polish their leadership skills.

They already spent so much time to define their vision, to understand their market, and to polish a solution. Some even have a list of goals, well-defined goals. That's a great start!

That was the first step, nothing but the first step. Now it is time to execute, to convert the ratios and the delays into teams and numbers.

Every single time that I met with a passionate entrepreneur, I smile and try my best to help them… but for that, they will have to listen first.

Bak is right at that crossroad. He already wrote many books and clearly defined his vision on stage and social media.

Very convincing in person, he has the chance and privilege to have financing without having to disclose all of his plans to the investors.

Bak is very creative and has a great team to support him. On the matter, everything that he lacks, his partner, Tranie Vo is taking over.

He is the visionary and the spokesperson. She is the builder and the bridge gaper. That's a great team; actually, that is the key ingredient to their success: clear vision and great management.

That team had great success in business for the last 15 years. They have built a significant enterprise with much growth potential.

Now it is time to jump into the major leagues. And playing in the major leagues, the rules are much, much different. This is where Bak surprised me.

You see, the longer an entrepreneur has spent time building his enterprise on his own, the more he/she has developed an ability to do thing their way and not to care about the opinions.

Eventually, he/she will reach a ceiling, just because they are doing things in a particular way.

Whatever mindset got them to where they are standing, is also shaping the glass ceiling refraining them from the next phase.

Meeting me is access to the next stage, and to play in the next step, one will have to learn to play with a different set of rules.

Can someone who succeeded with a mindset leave that one behind to start over with a different one, one much broader?

This is where some success will remain small and will never grow into the company they could have. It is a matter of pride and mindset.

To move up into the major leagues, one will have to forget about his/her past victories, skills, and mindset.

One will have to be willing to move on and leave everything that he/she knew behind, moving forward with nothing but his/her confidence and his/her will. It will take more than just ambition and will to keep pride at bay.

Bak has spent enough time to discover himself and to practice his entrepreneurship skills.

Now it is time for him to learn to build and master big structures, those he will need to materialize his vision. His gift is the way that he sees the world!

From his track record, he has proven that he can manage ambition and stress. His luck is that he is open to learn and to relearn. Furthermore, he can recognize quickly what he does not know.

"The challenge is to balance audacity, stubbornness, and Open-mindedness."
Christian Trudeau

This is where Bak captivated my attention. Very confident and acknowledgeable, Bak is also among the most open-minded people that I have met. Very audacious, he has show flexibility of mind and action that surprised me.

I asked him for a **Strategical Plan** in writing. He told me without hesitation that he didn't have one. I like the man and his vision, but for me to help him, I needed something to build from. By the time that I proposed to him my help to make one, he has completed one on his own.

It was a draft of the whole vision of the **Mdex group**. Not perfect and still merely a selection, the result was quite stunning. It was a good draft on which to refine and build from.

The organization is a science, not an art. It is a series of logical steps that add up one to the other, forming a whole greater than the sum.

The order and chronology of the steps and how they interact with one another are of prime importance.

To master the process, one needs experience and skills, but like everything else, it can be learned.

What Bak proved that day is that he is ready to learn, once more. I did not have to convince him, I asked, he took the time to make up his mind between the past (solo) or the future (to open up) and today, we are writing, not only a book but the future in dialogue together.

"A plan is worth a thousand words.
An Organizational Matrix is worth
a thousand plans."
Christian Trudeau

This is **HUMAN FACTOR** for **MILLION DOLLAR MINDSET.**

GIVE YOURSELF THE MEANS OF YOUR VISION.
THIS TIME, STAY IN THE BOX, MASTER THE BOX

Dr. BAK NGUYEN

CHAPTER 17

THE RECRUITMENT
FROM CHANGING THE WORLD FROM A
DENTAL CHAIR

by Dr. BAK NGUYEN

I have included this chapter about talent management because soon enough, you will have to face the building and management of a team.

With the Organizational Structure of Christian Trudeau borrowed from **HUMAN FACTOR**, you have a way to bridge between budgeting and recruiting. And usually, hiring will boost your income.

So if the main subject of this book was to build a successful business plan, your success would bring you soon enough to manage a team.

Far from a walk in the park, I can tell you that Human Resources is a field on its own and will require much time and skill to excel in.

Since the theme of this book was **SUCCESSFUL**, why not? Why not include for you a chapter of

TALENTS MANAGEMENT and the philosophy that I apply to my team and staff.

From the same book written to defend my nomination as Ernst & Young Entrepreneur of the Year, **CHANGING THE WORLD FROM A DENTAL CHAIR**, I am borrowing the chapter of **TALENTS MANAGEMENT**.

Based on 15 years plus of experience from the field. I must also add a precision, and this book has been written almost a year before I wrote **HUMAN FACTOR** with my mentor Christian Trudeau. I've learned much since.

I've learned and adapted... In other words, I've evolved. I found it interesting for you to appreciate the evolution and the difference within a year on the field.

I told you that business is a constant effort of adaptation. Here's the exciting part: I still stand by everything that I wrote in **CHANGING THE WORLD FROM A DENTAL CHAIR**, but I have grown much since, and I keep evolving, that's the fun in the game.

HUMAN FACTOR is the next stage of my evolution as a CEO. That being said, the point I wanted to make here is that you are about to be in a position of power. With power comes responsibilities (as the friendly neighborhood hero said).

You are leading a team. With time and success, your team will grow into a community. It is your duty to lead the team and to see that each member have a chance to evolve to reach his/her full potential.

The previous chapter covered how to build a team on paper. This one will cover how to live with a team daily. In a sense, I will quote Tony Hsieh, CEO, and founder of **Zappos** and author of **DELIVERING HAPPINESS**: to manage a company is a little like to social experiment on a micro-community.

And before you misunderstood the meaning of the words, Mr. Hsieh is looking for more and more ways to share with his staff. The social experiments were all to improve the relationship of a team member to relate to the company.

So you too will be responsible for the lives of those you chose to work for you. Be honest and respectful, and do not forget who you are! You are the leader, that's your new role now!

I am nothing without my team. But I've also learned to have the capability to recruit new team members as I go on my journey. I did mention that gratitude and loyalty are traits that I embody and look forward to.

My first entrepreneurial endeavor as a movie producer taught me the value of loyalty, loyalty to the people and the project that I served.

Unfortunately, that does not always include the people I serve with. I am the kind of man that is looking for friendship and brotherhood before looking for a business partner.

" People change, you change, respect that and deal with it."

Dr. Bak Nguyen

As I will always give the credit when it is due and accept my wrongs when it's the case. I hold my team dear to me, but I do not own the people on my side, nor do they own me. I am an agent of change, that's the only certitude and the only thing that may not change.

It is not reasonable to expect most people to keep up with me nor to keep the same drive year after year after year. So I learned to respect everyone, their ambitions, and their limits. I ask for the same in return that they respect me for who I am today and who I will become tomorrow.

That's why I am always happy to welcome a new team member, a patient, or a partner. As time goes by, things will change, and eventually, we will part ways, sometimes in functional terms, sometimes not. It is unfortunate, and I try my best to honor the good memories rather than the bad ones.

That's also why I will never hold back someone from leaving **Mdex** to go to his/her next phase in life. I haven't always been like this, but experience taught me not to get attached.

Nothing good will come out of a relationship that was meant to end and that you keep artificially alive. Ever watched Stephen King's Pet Cemetery?

At **Mdex**, I have mainly two teams: the clinical team and the corporate team. The corporate team is the team responsible for most of the development and innovation at **Mdex & Co**, **Mdex Industries,** and **Mdex V**.

Except for myself and my co-founder, partner, and wife, Tranie Vo, most of the team members are partners that we recruited from other industries. I told you that I wanted a fresh look.

From IT engineering to dental engineering, most of my VPS own their own company and have decided to join forces with us.

Banks officers, landlords, lawyers firms, tax advisors, accounting firms, architects and designer firms, all have become partners at some level and are vital parts of the **Mdex group**.

Even my mentor, Dr. Jean De Serres, former president of Hema-Quebec, is starting to think that **Mdex** is growing from his influence. I love the man for that, for his wisdom, his friendship, and his faith in me.

I have the chance to have counsellors like the former general director of Telus, Tee Tran, the man who brought all the animals to Telus and was at the wheel of bringing Clearnet to Telus as one of Canada's biggest companies.

When you look at most of those relationships, the common thread is friendship, respect... and ambition. We share the same vibe, and we empower one another.

That is the all-star team that I have the privilege to work with. I thank each of them for their trust and support.

Partners, not employees, even if there is an exchange of money! Of course, the basis of respect is to recognize your partner at his/her valid value.

Within my inner circle, I also have the chance of having three counsellors, a Diplomatic Counsellor, a Medical Counsellor, and an International Counsellor.

They are responsible for all the diplomacy and negotiation with the outside, the other companies, countries, organizations, and governments.

That might seem exhaustive, but since the launch of **Mdex & Co** and its new divisions, proposals of partnerships and business are coming daily from all over the planet.

Under the direction of my most trusted partner and officer, Tranie Vo, my Vice President of business development, we are driving together **Mdex** into the new age of dentistry.

My clinical team is an excellent team of professionals all dedicated to the well-being of my patients. Their focus is mainly aimed at the patient level, not at the "cosmic" standard as they like to qualify my ambitions and projects.

That team has changed over the years, and we learned to include everyone while keeping on expanding and recruiting new members.

Except for dentists, all of them are employees and vibrate at another level. Not better, not worst, different. Also, except for dentists, most of them are from diverse educational backgrounds.

I am someone who does not care much about the credentials. I look for value and personal worth. With the years, I have come to realize that not everyone can vibrate at my frequency. Maybe for a little while, but most won't last for a long time.

Credentials, value, and education are all factors that will tell me how long someone will share their journey with me.

I said before that I am thankful to have been accepted as one of their own as a Canadian, as a Quebecker, as a dentist. But as an entrepreneur and a visionary, I have, at times, isolated myself by my own doing.

It took me much time and wisdom to accept that reality, and twenty years as an entrepreneur has led me to let go, to appreciate my team for who they are, to empower them, to enjoy the time we have together and to wish them to luck the day they'll decide to move to new horizons.

Partners are the same, but usually, they are sharing the same vibe, ambition, and level of education. In other words, often, the relationship lasts longer, and my growth empowers their growth.

" Connections instead of comparisons.
That's the key."
Dr. Bak Nguyen

I am well surrounded, but I know that the team will change. If I want to be able to lead Mdex to the new era of my industry, that's the only way to go.

That's why I have built my focus on forging structure and policy, tools, and environment, more than focusing on a particular person and developing that human trust.

I get pretty close with the people I work with, but I do not work with all members of the clinical team nor the expansion team.

Even to my patients, I am loyal and will remain their attending dentist, but I also need to find them other dentists that I trust, so their needs are met in timely fashion, always with the **Mdex's** touch.

It's about transition and structure. That's the role of the leader: to see the big picture and to lead his team; his team, not all the individuals working in the company.

"Mdex is neither the staff nor the dentist.
If Mdex is someone, Mdex is the patient!"
Dr. Bak Nguyen

When I said that at a staff meeting three years ago, I almost risked my life! And I do not blame them. I was honest with them, but since we do not vibrate at the same frequency nor see life the same way, it was foolish of myself to share that thought with them.

I was being respectful by treating them the same way I wanted to be treated, with the truth.

"There is no absolute truth. The truth is not the same for people of different vibes and values."

Dr. Bak Nguyen

Do I have any regrets? No, no one ever taught me how to lead, I learned with my partner, Tranie Vo, on the field. Would I do things differently today? Sure, but I needed the experience first to acquire wisdom.

To all past **Mdex** members, I wish you luck and the best of what you want to for. That being said, I have learned to remove the entrance gate of my company. Most people are welcome to join. Everything is merit-based, and promotion will follow accordingly.

Mdex is an ever-changing model; my structures and policies are also built keeping flexibility and growth in mind.

Nothing is set in stone, and nothing will last forever. Every day, we need to renew our commitment to the patient, to the future, to each other.

This is undoubtedly an unorthodox approach to human resources. As I said before, I do not pretend that **Mdex** has the perfect recipe, just the groundworks on which we could all evolve and build from, as you chose to grow. **Mdex** is and will always be that way.

"Loyalty is to a commitment, not to a person."
Dr. Bak Nguyen

With many scars and failures in this sector, I have grown pretty good at attracting talents. That's right, and we invite people to us.

Sometimes, if I see a particular person, someone that I share a vibe with, I reach out... it's often them who reach out first. I manage to keep honesty and respect at the heart of each relationship.

I've also learned not to ask for perfection; since I am not perfect myself, I will not put that burden on anyone. So if you ask me: how do I recruit? By attraction.

If you ask me: how do I incentivize people working with me? I inspire. How do I identify talent? Based on merit. How do I get along with people? By feeling a good vibe! That's **Mdex**.

Make it happen. This is the **MILLION DOLLAR MINDSET.**

GIVE YOURSELF THE MEANS OF YOUR VISION
THIS TIME, STAY IN THE BOX, MASTER THE BOX.

Dr. BAK NGUYEN

CHAPTER 18
THE MOMENTUM
FROM SELMADE
by Dr. BAK NGUYEN

From writing a business plan, we went pretty far. The theme of **SUCCESS** brought you to draft your **BUSINESS PLAN** and **WEBSITE**, only to start over with expert who will bring your vision and presentation to the next level.

With a great business plan, you have your foot at the door. Now put the business plan aside and expose yourself to the questioning and the challenge. Are being interviewed for the title of **CEO** and **FOUNDER** of a **NEW CORPORATION**.

Then, I shared with you what I learned from my mentor Christian Trudeau: converting a business plan into a team, delays, and ratios.

I even covered the field of recruitment and team management, maybe not in-depth but enough to get you informed and hungry to learn more.

"The real danger is to ignore what we don't know."

Dr. Bak Nguyen

So keep learning and asking questions, your journey has just begun, you are now in business. Small league, big league, some rules are universal. And the first universal rule that I learned is: **YOU ARE AS GOOD AS YOU LAST WIN**.

In other words, for as long as you are right and have the numbers to prove it, your team and your partners will stand behind you. But the day that you are showing weakness (lost), your trial will begin.

Don't get any ideas, and this will happen, sooner or later, it will happen. We are swimming against the tide and are creating the future, safe is not part of the journey.

The way you will react and manage, but the failure and the street will make or break you. So be prepared for the worst while hoping for the best.

That being said, would you like a take of my mindset to keep the worst at bay and the hope high? Allow me to ease your way to victory and success!

I will borrow a chapter of **SELFMADE**, my 35th book to share with you ways and philosophy to keep winning, despite the odds.

May **MOMENTUM** be with you.

HOW TO KEEP THE STREAK OF WINS UP

FROM SELF-MADE
CHAPTER 8
by Dr. BAK NGUYEN

"ASK YOURSELF DO YOU LIKE TO WIN
MORE THAN YOU ARE SCARED TO FAIL."

Dr. Bak Nguyen

I started this book telling you that entrepreneurship is not a profession but a philosophy. It's our **attitude** toward *Life* and people.

It is how we choose to see and to embrace the day, rainy and cloudy and walk until the sun is behind us without us noticing it.

In the last chapter, I told you that my millionaire status helped me when I started. It gave me a goal to walk toward to. Well, I went so far beyond the arrival line when I realized that I had achieved my goal.

And guess what? I was too busy working on the present matter to burden myself with words and adjectives.

I wasn't the same man anymore. I've changed, I've evolved. What I did to reach that stage was to work on myself and to develop my **skillset** and **attitude**.

"The keys to victory are skill set and attitude."
Dr. Bak Nguyen

Both of them matter. Please, do not confuse the terms. A skill set is something you trained over and over for until you've mastered it.

It is a **HOW TO** that's now part of your reflexes and nature. It's part of your intelligence, logic, and disciple. I dedicated my first book on the matter, **SYMPHONY OF SKILLS**.

On the other hand, an **attitude** is your **EMOTIONAL INTELLIGENCE** in action. This is **HOW** you react to events, things, and people. Like skills, it can be trained, but it is part of a whole different realm, the emotional realm.

The common mistake I noticed is that most people ignore their emotions. They try to bury them and to act simply with logic.

It might work for a little while, until their feelings come bursting out and reverse, even destroy everything they stood for until there.

"Don't run from your emotions.
They are from your heart, and
your heart is bigger than
your brain."
Dr. Bak Nguyen

Let me repeat that: your heart is more significant than your brain! Ever heard the saying that we only use 10% of our mind? Trust me, and if you were using 50% of your heart, you'd be dead!

The sooner you accept it, the better you'll be. Otherwise, it's yourself that you are fighting.

There is no victory possible here, no upside and no gain. Still not convinced that your **ATTITUDES** are more significant than your **SKILLS**?

In the stock market, what are the fundamentals? To buy low and to sell high. Pretty simple, right? So why is it that so few people succeed for a long time? Because the **EMOTIONS** are reversed to the **LOGIC** in that scheme.

The stocks market is first and foremost a place of people, **GREED** and **FEAR**, in other words, of **EMOTIONS**.

To go in thinking that you can survive only with logic and numbers is the best way to be served as profit to the market itself!

When the prices are low, that means that people are dropping the title, they are running from a sinking ship, will you run in and buy, with enthusiasm?

You are scared to death and buying seems like the last thing you want to do. That's what it means to buy low.

When the price soars, why don't you sell? Because of the minute you sell, the price just got even higher!

Then, you feel like you just missed out on an opportunity that you've sold yourself short. That's the **EMOTIONAL** part of you, your **attitude**. Can you deny your nature?

"Carve out your heart and throw it away.
Sounded stupid? And yet that's
what we are trained to do."
Dr. Bak Nguyen

No heart, no Power.

No heart, no Passion.

No heart, no Hope.

No heart, no Heat

No Heat, no Energy

No Energy, no Life

This is true to everyone, but to you, entrepreneurs, it is of prime importance since you are always in action.

Your philosophy, your attitude, and your skills are the actions paving the ladders of life, on a daily pace. And since your actions serve a public, all those people are somehow under your influence.

That, you already know. Your responsibility goes further than your actions since you influence people's life, will you be spreading **FEAR** or **HOPE**?

You read right, **FEAR,** or **HOPE**. Whatever you are providing is a mean, a solution to solve the future, of what is ahead. If you were deeply rooted in the experience, the past and what is well-proven, you are perpetuating and promoting the **INSURANCE**. In other words, you are mirroring **FEAR**…

If you are standing for the new and are reinventing Life as an artist, you are showing the world from a new perspective, your perspective, you are embracing **HOPE**.

This is not just philosophical nor a rhetorical exercise. In both situations, your **attitude** is the mirror of your emotions and how you are reacting to the world. That's energy, that's the vibe.

"Nothing is more contagious than energy since we are always thirsty for it."
Dr. Bak Nguyen

So how all of this can ensure a win? If you finally understood that your heart is more significant than your head, listen to your emotions, and free them.

Of course, it will be messy, ever try to free a stallion in a living room? Your emotions need freedom and space to run, but once it has circled the perimeter, it will come back to you, ready to be tamed.

"Give yourself the time and space to be."
Dr. Bak Nguyen

Learn to understand them and play with them. In my 15th book, **FORCES OF NATURE**, I painted how each of us can leverage on our emotions.

"Emotion is the beast inside of us.
We can mount it or be eaten by it."
Dr. Bak Nguyen

Only whole, with both your heart and your head you may find happiness. And once happy, nothing can stand in your way. You will always find an idea, a new way. That's the hope, that's the attitude.

Not just yours, but also the attitude of most people whom you inspired. Your vibe spreads freely, and those open to you will be empowered and lifted by it.

That's your responsibility to lead your people to happiness. You are a leader, accept it, respect it.

"Do you like to win more
than you are scared to fail?"
Dr. Bak Nguyen

On the other hand, you can sell **FEAR** and feed on people's weakness. That works too. That's how you may sell the most.

But here's the catch: the *vibe* goes both ways, and since you are a mirror of your *attitudes*, you are bathing in the same crap that you are selling.

Goods, words, ideas, it does not matter; the principle is the same, **HOPE** or **FEAR**, **PAST** or **FUTURE**. You can't be both, and you will have to choose your philosophy and your nature.

Use the words, and they will be. That's as simple as that. Love to win and you are embracing *hope* and the *future*… for as long as we are talking about future wins.

Fear to fail and never will you have a chance to prove yourself and to find out what you are made of. Concern for too long and you are building a *psychological wall* from the *unknown*, from the *future*.

"Behind the walls, you will grow roots and thoughts, but you've lost your horizon."
Dr. Bak Nguyen

So really, it is not just a matter of choice but one of the consequences. Do you let yourself be motivated by **FEAR** or by **HOPE**?

Are you more fearful of losing than you love winning? Choose carefully since you will become what you choose and say. Consider yourself warned.

"Have the right mindset, and you will redefine your reality and the world with it."
Dr. Bak Nguyen

Have discipline and train to master your skills to put into action your views and emotions. Listen to your feelings, let them run free and learn to leverage from them, that's your best shot to success.

I learned to mount my beast, my feelings… And my beast is a **tornado**.

"Speed is my power."
Dr. Bak Nguyen

If you really want to know, that's exactly how I made it, I got through, how I went beyond. I told you at the beginning of this book that I achieved more within the last 18 months than I've done in the previous 40 years.

Of course, I built from what was and found leverage on the Past. But I was also keen enough not to be trapped by the Past, the insurances, and the experiences. My *hopes* are big, and I managed to push my fears to another world…

Those of you who are looking into how I mounted my beast and became a **MOMENTUM**, I have shared my views and recipes with coach Dino Masson in my 8th book, **MOMENTUM TRANSFER**.

We went it deep into it, breaking down the step to build and to feed a **MOMENTUM**.

"The fear of God keeps me going
without hesitation."
Dr. Bak Nguyen

I accepted who I am and embraced *Life*,

Betting on myself.

Hard, fun, easy and treacherous,

Life is like a box of chocolate…

But whatever I get,

I chew, sometimes I eat and swallow.

Other times, I spit it out.

It is what it is.

All I can do

Is to make the most

And the best of every situation.

That's the attitude.

To move forward and to, one day, face God, I learned to leave the burdens behind. The principles, the values, the judgments, all those preconceived ideas of how the world acts behind the wall…

Out in the *canvas of Life*, there is no right or bad, just purposes and means.

"We are animals who learned to sing."
Dr. Bak Nguyen

That's our ways to express ourselves and our emotions. Animals with emotions, nothing more, nothing less. My life is my journey to discover and to enjoy.

In my case, I had to go beyond the wall to start my real journey. The minute I was on the other side, I realized that all that I knew, all that I hold dear, all that I feared, nothing has the same weight on the other side of the wall.

Looking at the future and the horizon, the rules changes, and the Past gained in perspective while it lost in size.

Actually whatever you look at for a long time will gain in perspective, so choose carefully on what you set your sight too. I could go on and on, but I covered all of those within **LEADERSHIP**, my 4th book, and **HYBRID**, my 12th book.

"The longer you look at something,
the more perspective it will gain.
You and your time are what giving
perspective to things,
events, and people."
Dr. Bak Nguyen

Entrepreneurship is a philosophy and a *choice of life* – a choice of *attitudes*, of *values*, of *worth*. Find your worth serving other people, and you will never run out of time. Find your speed listening to the beast inside, and you will mount your emotions to surf on the **waves of Life**.

Embrace your heart

Make your head bow to your Hopes

You'll be writing your legend

History is not made with words

But with footsteps and footnotes

Legends grow into a movement

By sharing, not with secrecy.

As you open your heart to Life,

You will see Hope.

You will feel hopeful.

You will be Hope.

And Hope is abundant and kind.

It is for you to decide your attitude

Only you can choose your philosophy

And you alone can draft your destiny

This is **SELFMADE** from **MILLION DOLLAR MINDSET.**

Dr. BAK NGUYEN

CONCLUSION

by Dr. BAK NGUYEN

I think that without a doubt we can be proud of ourselves. Together we've been through a great journey.

Yours, the real one is awaiting ahead. Looking back, I should have titled this book: **THE MAKING OF THE CEO** or **THE FATE OF THE ENTREPRENEUR**.

But I stick with my original title, **HOW TO WRITE A SUCCESSFUL BUSINESS PLAN** for the only reason that I want you to have something concrete and palpable after this journey. One you can hold in your hand and leverage on.

How many times have I seen people motivate and excited at the end of a seminar, only to meet them a few years down the road and to recognize the same lost eyes I met before.

The excitement was gone, and they are back looking for new motivation. But nothing else.

"Actions, people,
Actions, are the ladders
to success."
Dr. Bak Nguyen

Do not let doubt and procrastination kill your dream or slow you down. I can't stretch it enough; you need action.

You've learned to **identify** a **need** and a **market**. I've shown you how I did it myself. You've then learned to build a **WEBSITE** within the hours, for as long as your ideas were bright. If not, this is time to address them.

Then, from the website, I showed ways to **test with minimum risks your market**. If all you wanted to do was to write a business plan, following my instructions, you now have a presence on the web. In other words, you are in business!

Then you followed me into the boardroom, those of the **decision-makers**. You know that all that you've done were merely a preparation for what's to come. In the room, it is now about you, all about who you are and what could you become.

Embrace the opportunity and shine! From the boardroom, I shared with you my relationship with the other side, the banks, bringing you the story of my banker, Rouba Sakr.

For the first time in the history of business books about **WRITING A BUSINESS PLAN**, you will have the entire story of how a business is and should be written.

I could have stopped there, but our journey was going so well, I didn't cut it short. So I went on with **PART III**, giving an inside of how I am applying those principles in my business. I borrowed chapters of my other books to prove my point.

Doing so allowed you to have a broader with of what it means to be a **CEO**. Just like me, you will be changing skin and taking on the next phase of your evolution, one tied to your business.

I strongly encourage you all to identify your strengths and weaknesses and to bet accordingly.

Yes, business is a bet, a gamble if you must. But we are not going in blind. There are ways to diminish the risks and to keep only the opportunities.

I will take this opportunity to remind you never to cut corners or to be cheap with those steps. These are the core of your business, so find the time and the resources to do it right. Cutting corners here is too expansive even to consider the option.

In the same line of thoughts, find the right experts to support and empower your vision. I was pretty proud when I wrote in a day the business plan of all three divisions of **Mdex**. Then, Christian told me to hire experts to polish it.

They redid most of the work and the calculations, even if the spine remains the same, the feeling and professionalism changed everything.

I have to thank Isabelle Maheux, our expert, who did a fantastic job delivering the plan that will reform an entire industry.

Between the business plan and the **ORGANIZATIONAL MATRIX**, we are rewriting part of the world with our minds and enthusiasm. I share them in here with you, since I am sure this is not a farewell. Our path will cross again, and, I am sure, sooner rather than later.

On that, I wish to you all, from the bottom of my heart, that you found your spark and idea and that this journey has empowered you to believe and to start gathering support.

That is the main point of a business plan, is to prep you to gather support, funds, and people to materialize your ideas and your views.

The world is evolving and becoming better thanks to dreamers like you and I. We are the builders and the pillars of evolution. We count on you and do not forget; you do not have to stand alone, not anymore.

Feel secure about sharing your ideas, be confident enough to grow those ideas, and you will be writing history and your destiny.

Entrepreneurs, my brothers and sisters in arms, I thank you for your passion and dedication. Entrepreneurs, I salute you.

Have you finished your business plan yet?

This is the **MILLION DOLLAR MINDSET.**

Dr. BAK NGUYEN

EAX

A new way to learn and enjoy Audiobooks. Made to be entertaining while keeping the self-educational value of a book, EAX will appeal to both auditive and visual people. EAX is the blockbuster of the Audiobooks.

EAX will cover most of Dr. Bak's books, and is now negotiating to bring more authors and more titles to the EAX concept.

Now streaming on Spotify, Apple Music and available for download on all major music platforms. Give it a try today!

EAX

TOTAL
IMMERSION WITH
ENHANCED AUDIO EXPERIENCE

Streaming Audiobook Blockbuster

Search for Dr. Bak Nguyen on SPOTIFY, Apple Music
and all major music platforms

FROM THE SAME AUTHOR
Dr. Bak Nguyen

TITLES AVAILABLE AT

www.DrBakNguyen.com

BUSINESS

La Symphonie des Sens
ENTREPREUNARIAT
par DR BAK NGUYEN

Industries Disruptors
BY DR. BAK NGUYEN, ROUBA SAKR AND COLLABORATORS

Changing the World from a dental chair
BY DR. BAK NGUYEN

The Power Behind the Alpha
BY TRANIE VO & DR. BAK NGUYEN

SELFMADE
GRATITUDE AND HUMILITY
BY DR. BAK NGUYEN

CHAMPION MINDSET
LEARNING TO WIN
BY DR. BAK NGUYEN & CHRISTOPHE MULUMBA

FACTEUR HUMAIN
LE LEADERSHIP DU SUCCÈS
par DR BAK NGUYEN & CHRISTIAN TRUDEAU

ehappyPedia
THE RISE OF THE UNICORN
BY DR. BAK NGUYEN & DR. JEAN DE SERRES

BRANDING DR.BAK
BALANCING STRATEGY AND EMOTIONS
BY DR. BAK NGUYEN, BRENDA GARCIA & SANTIAGO CHICA

CHILDREN'S BOOK
with William Bak

The Trilogy of Legends

THE LEGEND OF THE CHICKEN HEART
BY DR. BAK NGUYEN & WILLIAM BAK

THE LEGEND OF THE LION HEART
BY DR. BAK NGUYEN & WILLIAM BAK

THE LEGEND OF THE DRAGON HEART
BY DR. BAK NGUYEN & WILLIAM BAK

WE ARE ALL DRAGONS
BY DR. BAK NGUYEN & WILLIAM BAK

THE 9 SECRETS OF THE SMART CHICKEN
BY DR. BAK NGUYEN & WILLIAM BAK

THE SECRET OF THE FAST CHICKEN
BY DR. BAK NGUYEN & WILLIAM BAK

THE LEGEND OF THE SUPER CHICKEN
BY DR. BAK NGUYEN & WILLIAM BAK

THE STORY OF THE CHICKEN SHIT
BY DR. BAK NGUYEN & WILLIAM BAK

WHY CHICKEN CAN'T DREAM?
BY DR. BAK NGUYEN & WILLIAM BAK

MILLION DOLLAR MINDSET

MOMENTUM TRANSFER
BY DR. BAK NGUYEN & Coach DINO MASSON

LEVERAGE
COMMUNICATION INTO SUCCESS
BY DR. BAK NGUYEN AND COLLABORATORS

THE POWER OF YES
MY 18 MONTHS JOURNEY
BY DR. BAK NGUYEN

HOW TO WRITE A BOOK IN 30 DAYS
BY DR. BAK NGUYEN

POWER
EMOTIONAL INTELLIGENCE
BY DR. BAK NGUYEN

MENTORS
BY DR. BAK NGUYEN

HOW TO NOT FAIL AS A DENTIST
BY DR. BAK NGUYEN

HOW TO WRITE A SUCCESSFUL BUSINESS PLAN
BY DR. BAK NGUYEN & ROUBA SAKR

MINDSET ARMORY
BY DR. BAK NGUYEN

PARENTING

THE BOOK OF LEGENDS
BY DR. BAK NGUYEN & WILLIAM BAK

THE BOOK OF LEGENDS 2
BY DR. BAK NGUYEN & WILLIAM BAK

HYBRID
THE MODERN QUEST OF IDENTITY
BY DR. BAK NGUYEN

FORCES OF NATURE
FORGING THE CHARACTER OF WINNERS
BY DR. BAK NGUYEN

SOCIETY

LEADERSHIP
PANDORA'S BOX
BY DR. BAK NGUYEN

KRYPTO
TO SAVE THE WORLD
BY DR. BAK NGUYEN & ILYAS BAKOUCH

LE RÊVE CANADIEN
D'IMMIGRANT À MILLIONNAIRE
par DR BAK NGUYEN

HORIZON, BUILDING UP THE VISION
VOLUME ONE
BY DR. BAK NGUYEN

HORIZON, ON THE FOOTSTEP OF TITANS
VOLUME TWO
BY DR. BAK NGUYEN

TITLES AVAILABLE AT

www.DrBakNguyen.com

DR.

Bak Nguyen